THE JONETTE JEWELRY COMPANY (JJ)

CREATORS of WHIMSEY, DRAMA, and DETAIL in JEWELRY DESIGN and MORE

Barbara Roesch Rokow and Nancy Rozendal

The Jonette Jewelry Company
Copyright © 2025
All rights reserved.
Published by Red Penguin Books
Bellerose Village, New York
ISBN 978-1-63777-831-9 / 978-1-63777-832-6
No part of this book may be reproduced in any form or by any electronic or mechanical means, including information storage and retrieval systems, without written permission from the author, except for the use of brief quotations in a book review.
In-house illustrator, Alan Weimer.
Cover design by Alan Weimer

The authors would like to extend their deep appreciation to all the JJ employees that met with us and shared their memories of working for the Company. We are proud of this book, and it would not have been as interesting or informative without their input.

TABLE OF CONTENTS

PREFACE 5
I. ORIGINS 8
   A. THE EARLY YEARS 8
   B. THE NEXT GENERATION 12
      GORDON LISKER 12
      DAVID LISKER 16

   C. IT TAKES A VILLAGE 18
      ALAN WEIMER 18
      JANET PARKER PRATA 25
      STEVE VALLONE 26
      HELEN NASUTA 30
      BRUCE McCOWAN 33
      RAPHAEL LOPES 35
      DIANE SANTOS 42

II.   A HAPPY REUNION 45
III. THE MANUFACTURING PROCESS 46
IV.   CURRENT PRICING 53
V.   ADVERTISING 54
VI.   VARIETY OF DESIGN THEMES 72
VII. LEGAL ISSUES 75
VIII. JJ'S CLAIM TO FAME - RECOGNITION OF JJ'S ARTISTRY BY JEWELRY PROFESSIONALS AND CELEBRITIES 77
IX.   PROVIDENCE, RHODE ISLAND-THE JEWELRY DISTRICT 79
X.   RECOGNIZING PROVIDENCE'S RICH JEWELRY HERITAGE – THE PROVIDENCE JEWELRY MUSEUM 81
XI.   DATING JONETTE JEWELRY 83
XII. THE BIG SELLERS 86

XIII.	HUMOR IN DESIGN	90
XIV.	EXAMPLES OF JJ CREATIONS WITH SOME ARTIST RENDERINGS	91
	CHRISTMAS AND RELIGION	156
	MISCELLANEOUS	183
XVI.	CONCLUSION	207

INDEX OF SKETCHES 209
INDEX OF JJ PHOTOS 217

THE JONETTE JEWELRY (J.J.) COMPANY- CREATORS OF WHIMSEY, DRAMA AND DETAIL IN JEWELRY DESIGN, AND MORE

PREFACE

What makes a costume jewelry reference book interesting? What makes a reader want to read the text and not just jump to the pictures, or at least go back to the text after looking at the pictures? A good story! Hopefully this book will provide the reader with an interesting and informative story of a classic American dream- come- true -immigrants from Russia who created wonderful costume jewelry and related products with a manufacturing operation that endured for decades. Jonette Jewelry Company, commonly referred to as "JJ", grew as a result of the ambition and hard work of its founder and father, Abraham Lisker, sons, Gordon and David, and the creativity, camaraderie, and dedication of its employees.

The reader is invited to follow the Liskers as they navigated family, the business culture of Providence, Rhode Island, and the hope and possibilities of the postwar environment. Early chapters describe the origin of Jonette and the challenges faced by all involved. Gordon and David's contributions to the huge success of JJ, as well as the significant roles executed by employees, including in-house designer, Alan Weimer and many others, are described and exemplified by sketches and photos of finished pieces.

Actual manufacturing processes, pricing, and marketing strategies and techniques are briefly described with samples of catalog items and the design themes with their stories. Many pins received recognition by jewelry professionals and celebrities. Due to the popularity and extensive national and international exposure of JJ pins, many designs were copied or "knocked off" as the industry referred to the travesty, and Gordon needed to act to protect his products. On occasion, the company had to deal with the opposite legal issue, threatened lawsuits against them such as a cease and desist order from Jim Henson, creator of the Muppets.

Information is also provided to the reader describing the difficulty dating the jewelry and some of Jonette's best selling items are identified. JJ made jewelry that was affordable and interesting. The vast array of designs is enormous, from mythological creatures such as dragons and wizards, to highly detailed wildlife and domestic animals including wolves, panthers, cats, dogs and beavers. JJ made brooches targeted to specific professions, such as real estate agents, teachers, artists and nurses. They made sophisticated cloud and moon pins, Egyptian themed pins and fairies. There was a separate Southwestern line called Santa Fe that included coyotes, cactus, desert scenes, and a wolf howling at the moon.

Throughout these pages you will find endless areas of interest; the seasons, including flowers, leaves and scenery for Spring; palm trees, fruit, and drinks for Summer; trees and pumpkins for Fall; and snow-covered trees for Winter. The jungle is represented with panthers, lions, tigers, giraffes, zebras, monkeys, and apes. Some of the birds included are flamingoes, eagles, pelicans, geese, ducks, chickadees, hummingbirds and swans. There are insects and butterflies and various woodland creatures. Frolicking with mermaids against a backdrop of the sea and lighthouses, whales, sea-rays and seahorses can be found. Reptiles creep amongst the collection-snakes, turtles and a gator whose jaw opens to reveal a bird inside! Frogs, salamanders and toads are some of the amphibians that don't want to be outshone by the reptiles. And the list goes on, including holiday celebrations, fantasy, romance, travel, military and patriotic themes.

Author Roesch Rokow (Barbara) was inspired to learn and share more about JJ because, as an avid costume jewelry collector, she was fascinated by its myriad of designs. Attempting to learn more about this creative jewelry line, Roesch Rokow discovered that there was no comprehensive written literature available. Upon retirement, she reached out to the Lisker family to see if there was interest in having a book written about the company. Author Rozendal (Nancy), wife of JJ CEO Gordon Lisker (Gordon), responded positively, as she herself had contemplated writing a book about JJ. Barbara traveled from upstate New York, along with her two equally avid costume jewelry collecting sisters, to Providence, to meet Gordon and Nancy.

To jumpstart the process, Nancy provided complete access to the records and jewelry the couple retained after the company closed in 2006. She arranged for Barbara to meet with some of JJ's former employees who still live in the Providence area, who shared their stories and memories of working for JJ. She also coordinated a private tour by curator, Peter DiCristofaro, of what was then the temporary home of the Providence Jewelry Museum. At the time, there was an enormous display of domestic and wild cat pins manufactured by Jonette. After conducting interviews, copying some of JJ's records and taking lots of pictures, a first draft was created. Nancy had previously written an article about JJ for the Providence Jewelry Museum, and her stories, which are incorporated herein, have added dimension to JJ's history. After Barbara circulated the first draft, the co-authors continued their collaboration, editing information and fine-tuning the book, before turning it over to the wonderful staff at Red Penguin Publishing for professional editing and organizing. Barbara and Nancy found they worked very well together, and have formed a friendship that will endure past this book's publication!

Both Nancy and Barbara have attempted to provide a unique opportunity to look into the inner workings of a costume jewelry company when America, and in particular, Providence, Rhode Island, produced most of the costume jewelry in the world. Part of the enduring popularity of Jonette's merchandise is due to the fantastical, and often humorous designs from dragons with belly aches to pterodactyls hovering over city skylines. We believe that readers will be interested as collectors, vendors, or just lovers of American history. As you peruse the pages herein, we hope you marvel at the vast array of designs and get a chuckle or two from seeing some of the artists' creations.

I. ORIGINS

A. THE EARLY YEARS

The Jonette Jewelry story begins with the Lisker brothers, sons of Russian immigrants, John and Etta Lisker. The brothers, Hy, Nathan and Abe, all became involved in the jewelry business at some point. After graduating from Brown in 1933 with a major in pre-med, Abe decided to go into business-the millinery business. As that required travel, Abe's mother encouraged him to come back home, stay in Providence, and partner with a distant family member who was in the rhinestone business.

Front: Albert, Rosie, Hyman, Nathan; Rear: Freida, John, Etta, Abe

By the mid-30s, the partners parted ways and Abe founded the Providence Jewelry Company at 185 Eddy Street, Providence, Rhode Island, in 1935. In 1937, Abe's youngest brother, Nathan, joined the Company and it was re-named Lisker and Lisker. Brother-in-law Harold

Corris then became involved, mostly purchasing stones. Retail customers included Macy's, Jordan Marsh and Bloomingdales.

A costume jewelry lover, Lucille Tempesta, used to publish a newsletter called "Vintage Fashion and Costume Jewelry" In her publication, Volume 8, #3, Summer edition, 1998, she published an article on JJ, called, "Vigilance-Guarding the Past, Present and Future of Jonette Jewelry." The article's author[1] interviewed Abe Lisker. Abe was working for a company called White Metal Rolling and Stamping Company when he decided to strike out on his own, in the year 1935. The article states, "With well-finished rhinestone jewelry, a small area of rented space and a few employees, Providence Jewelry Company was born. Abraham Lisker had planted his feet on the path where he would spend all of his business life."

Abe was drafted in 1941 and the business closed. After a military medical discharge in 1944, Abe formed the Jonette Jewelry Company, combining his parents' names of John and Etta. Abe's brother, Hyman, joined the Company that same year. He oversaw the books and handled the Company's legal affairs. Eventually, JJ moved to 85 South Street in the middle of Providence's Jewelry District. In JJ's case, the location was conveniently located next to Regal Plating, a company with which JJ did business.

South Street, Providence

---

1   Vintage Fashion and Costume Jewelry, Volume 8, #13, Summer, 1998, by Lucille Tempesta (The particular author is not clear, but at the end of the article it states: "This article was written with the cooperation of Marcia Brown and the Lisker family. We thank them.")

In 1949, the brothers created another company, Reksil (Lisker, spelled backwards), which sold the same lines as JJ, but it used a separate salesperson who had to get his own client base. It isn't clear when Reksil closed. Steve Vallone, long time employee of JJ under both Abe and Gordon, speculates there were likely two primary reasons for the separate company-one, to expand customer base, and two, to take advantage of certain financial and tax considerations.

Abe expanded the business from the creation of turtle, ballerina, bird and Christmas tree pins to include silverware with mother of pearl handles. He sold to jobbers like Pakula and Thomas Long. The diversification of jewelry production to include non-jewelry items was novel, and Abe's direction started a new trend in the jewelry industry. Abe was respected for his honesty, hard work and quality production. JJ did well in the 50s and 60s, selling mainly "cute" painted goods that were both colorful and whimsical. They used mother of pearl in many of their animal pins, and "smoked pearl", which was a gray mother of pearl. Although the Company expanded into other manufacturing lines, its chief product was jewelry, primarily pins. More can be found regarding Abe in the section about long term employee, STEVE VALLONE on page 26.

Abe married Geraldine Gordon and had two sons, Gordon, born in 1944, and David, born in 1947. In the early 60's, Gordon left the Providence area to attend and graduate from Union College, take courses at Massachusetts College of Art, and pursue other interests including getting his real estate license. He returned around 1970, and joined the family business. But Abe was a tough taskmaster. Gordon had to turn on the gas-fired melting pots at 5:30 am, to melt the metal, so it would be ready for casting when the other employees came in. He also had to do sweeping, carding and wrapping. Fortunately for all, the gas-fired melting pots were subsequently set on automatic timers. Gordon was interested in design, but his father wanted him to focus on the business end of the operation. Ultimately, Gordon did both. His creativity drove JJ sales through the roof, while his business acumen kept the business running successfully for decades.

Gordon married co-author Nancy Rozendal. David married Marcia Blount, with whom he had two daughters, Livia and Alexia. David and Marcia subsequently divorced, and David married Elissa (Ellie) Tonkin.

Left to Right, standing, David Lisker with his daughters, Alexia and Livia, and former wife, Marcia Blount; seated, Nancy Rozendal and Gordon Lisker; Abe Lisker, seated, and his wife, Geraldine (Jerry) Lisker (standing).

By the late 1960s, Abe and brother, Hy, were ready for retirement and the business was operating with less than 20 employees. By 1972, both Abe and Hyman had retired, leaving Gordon to run the Company. Abe, though, never really never let go of his "baby", and kept going into the plant until the day before he died in 2002. Gordon rose to the challenge of continuing JJ's growth.

Gordon's first design is depicted to the left, a free form peace symbol. His father, however, had no use for the design and didn't produce it.

B. THE NEXT GENERATION

GORDON LISKER

CEO and President Gordon Lisker led the Jonette Jewelry Company with a strong work ethic, determination, humor and grace. As Vice President of Operations, Helen Nasuta, stated, Gordon also had the business acumen to "…surround himself with a pool of incredibly talented and dedicated employees." This included the designers, model makers, schedulers, organizers and marketers, who put in long hours as needed, particularly when it was time to get the new product lines ready for shows.

It was no easy task running a costume jewelry company that manufactured so many different designs, and in such large quantities. The best estimate is that JJ created between 18,000 and 20,000 designs over its history. In addition, JJ used several different finishes in the production of jewelry, from its classic pewter finishes, to gold tone and silver tone, both matte and shiny, bronze and brass, colorful enamels and more. The Company also incorporated faux pearls, mirrors, resin and rhinestones in some of its creations.

Although JJ is best known for its wide variety of pins, the Company made many other items over the years. They made necklaces, earrings, bolo ties, belt loops and zip pulls. There was also the manufacture of perfume bottles, figurines, letter openers, photo frames, bookmarks, mirrors, candle holders, card holders, clocks, spoons, napkin rings, magnets, boxes, magnifying glasses and sun visor clips. Examples of the breadth of JJ designs can be seen in its brochure that starts on page 50.

Gordon took great pride in assuring JJ maintained its reputation for creating quality products. It is quite a juxtaposition to see the chaos in his cluttered office with the precise and highly detailed pieces that were manufactured by the Company. Gordon's office was so cluttered that when he met with the designers, model makers and wholesalers, he would use the office showroom which was large, neat and organized

Gordon's Office

Gordon at Work

Caricature of Gordon done by a street artist, E.G. Mill, 1979, Wickford, RI Art Festival. Note the jewelry and cigar!

With the exception of the electroplating, every part of the manufacturing process was done in-house, and Gordon oversaw it all. Once approved by Gordon, two dimensional designs were passed to one of the model makers, including, among others, David Lisker, Jim Dumachelle, Tony Martins, Nunzio Izzo, Keith Curvelo, Janet Parker (1990s-2006) a/k/a Janet Parker Prata, Tom Marcello, Isaac Newar, Mike Manni, Richard Dickerson, Mike Guirino and Raphael Lopes. Almost all of the JJ designs came from Gordon's creative mind, and Gordon oversaw each item to completion. The Company's talented designers took Gordon's concepts and made them a reality, with their skilled artistic abilities.

An example of how Gordon valued his employees dates back to February 6, 1978, when Rhode Island had "THE GREAT BLIZZARD." It hit so hard and so fast, Gordon let everyone out of work, but already buses either weren't showing up or were already stuck. People who were supposed to be picked up weren't, as travel was treacherous. Gordon had a four wheel drive vehicle, but when he went to close the factory, he saw a few of the older female employees were out in front, waiting for some way to get home. He told them to get in and he'd take them. It was so bad, he barely made it to Nancy Rozendal's 2-family house on the Eastside. He couldn't get the women to North Providence where they were all from. All of them were snowed in at Nancy's apartment for 3 days. They cooked everything Nancy had, did all her mending, cleaned, and worried a lot about how they'd ever get home. Nancy's neighbors, and Gordon and Nancy finally shoveled THE STREET! On the fourth day, the ladies decided they would walk home - probably 4-5 miles. Gordon and Nancy weren't happy about it, but they all made it. Everyone had a lot of laughs and everything ended well. They loved Gordon!

By the late 80s, JJ needed more space. Gordon had grown the Company tremendously since he took over the helm, adding many more employees to meet expanded production needs. Gordon purchased 373 Taunton Ave, East Providence, to accommodate the growing company. The building was 18,000 square feet and had a parking lot. Jonette ultimately employed between 80 and 125 employees, including the talented in house designer, Alan Weimer. When Gordon first joined Jonette, there were only about 20 employees, and even less than that when he assumed the helm of the Company.

373 Taunton Avenue

DAVID LISKER

Around the mid-70s, Gordon's brother, David, joined the Company as a partner. He had a Masters in Business Administration from the University of Chicago. In addition to his business background, he brought his great imagination and artistic ability, which proved invaluable to Jonette. He worked in the Company until 1979, when he sold his share of the Company back to Gordon and explored other business opportunities.

He later returned to JJ in the 90s, working as a model maker and bringing the Company sorely needed computer expertise. Until he returned, the Company was not using computers in its operations, which seems incredible in today's computer dependent environment. He left Jonette around 2005 to start his own company, Brookline Pewtersmith, which made custom keychains. David was instrumental in organizing the closure of JJ in 2006. David passed away on April 25, 2017, after a long battle with lymphoma.

In the earlier cited Vintage Fashion and Costume Jewelry article[1] on JJ, the article states "In 1972, when his father retired, the Jonette Jewelry path was taken by Gordon, who found himself firmly entrenched as the new owner. Brother David a graduate of Wesleyan University with a business degree from the University of Chicago, took over the model making and became the compliance officer for all new state and federal business regulations." Long time employee Steve Vallone described David as very nice, and more of a worrier than Gordon.

1	Vintage Fashion & Costume Jewelry, Vol. 8, #3, Summer, 1998, Lucille Tempesta

JJ DESIGNERS AND MODEL MAKERS

There were so many talented model makers and designers that worked for JJ over the years, some in-house and some as independent contractors. The following is a list of many of those employees:

In House Designers:

AW	Alan Weimer(1970s-close)		A	Ann Donahue(mid 1990s)
M	Marion Firmani(1990s)		VS	Virginia (Ginny) Stevens(1990s)

Independent Contractor Designers:

JP	Janet Parker Prata (1990s-2006) a/k/a Janet Parker Prata		LG	Louis R. Guisti (late 1970s)
			CN	Chuck Noreau (mid 1970s)
VS	Virginia (Ginny) Stevens (1990s)		NI	Nunzio Izzo (1990s)
E	Eric Bergeran (mid 1990s)			

In House Model Makers

DL	David Lisker(1970s,1990s-early 2000s)		PB	Paul Baron(1977-1986)
			RD	Richard Dickerson(1990s)
R	Raphael Lopes(mid 1990s-close)		I	Isaac Newar(1990s)
K	Keith Curvelo(early 1990s-2006)		TM	Tony Martins (1990s-early 2000s)
J	Jim Dumachelle(1980s-early 2000s)		NI	Nunzio Izzo(1990s)(designer and model maker)

Independent Contractor Model Makers

MM	Mike Manni(1990s)		John	John Florio(1997)
D	Dan Salliby(2001)		FB	Frank Barberi(1970s-1980s)

We were lucky enough to reach some of the retired employees, who willingly shared their JJ experiences. Common themes that emerged from talking to those employees, was a love and respect for not only Gordon Lisker, but also for each other; pride in the products they helped create and bring to market, and satisfaction in knowing their hard work and creativity helped keep JJ a successful company for decades. They paint a picture of Gordon as hard working, generous and creative. Gordon had a deep voice, and a bad habit of running late to appointments, which some mistook for arrogance.

On the following pages, you will meet some of the Jonette Jewelry Company employees that helped make the Company so successful.

C. IT TAKES A VILLAGE...

ALAN WEIMER

Alan Weimer graduated from the School of Art at Virginia Commonwealth University with a major in Illustration. In 1973, he was hired as an apprentice designer at a company called Alan Jewelry. The two owners of the company were Allan Nason and Allen Owen. Over the next five years, Allen Owen taught him the basics of jewelry design, model making and the manufacturing processes of costume jewelry.

JJ was naturally dependent on having an excellent designer to bring the jewelry and other items "to life". Alan Weimer was Jonette's in-house, full-time artist, who Gordon hired in 1977. Alan said that Gordon was fun to work for, and that Gordon had a good sense of humor. Alan ultimately spent over 29 years working for Jonette. He created over 12,000 designs for the Company during his time there.

Alan worked with up to six in-house model makers at any given time, along with one free lance model maker, who would drop off a completed model and pick up a new design on a weekly basis. To draw an accurate design for a model maker to use, Alan would begin by doing quick sketches. He would then pick a sketch and place a sheet of tracing paper over it, and using a drafting pencil sharpened to a needle point, he slowly refined the lines until a clear and accurate drawing was achieved. Alan joked that there was a certain "Zen" to his drawing technique. He said that while concentrating on putting a line to paper, he would enter into something similar to a meditative state, as he watched the tip of his pencil create beautiful lines.

His, and the model makers' workspace, was a large corner room on the second floor of the Taunton Avenue factory, with high ceilings and six foot tall windows on two sides. "The north light was an artist's dream", he said, and "it was a lot like being in art class for 29 years, and art class was one of my favorites places."

Alan noted that unlike many of the other costume jewelry manufacturers who were fashion oriented and tracked the latest trends from New York and Paris, Jonette tracked the current trends in popular culture. Both Gordon and Alan looked for current developments in places like home décor magazines, items in the news, undercurrents in art and music, et cetera. In addition to the pop culture-related designs, holiday themed items were always a big part of the JJ line.

The two men collaborated on many designs. Gordon trusted Alan's aesthetic instincts, and basically gave him unlimited authority to create new lines. Whether a design originated with Gordon, Alan or someone else, Alan would work up a line drawing to show Gordon for final approval, or as Gordon said,…"to stick my two cents in". Generally, the designs originated with JJ employees and many design concepts came from Gordon. The Company did not usually get specific design requests from customers. A customer like Park Lane might ask for exclusivity to sell a JJ design, but the customer did not come up a specific design of its own.

This wonderful Egyptian pin bears both the names of JJ and Parklane

There were individuals and companies, however, for which JJ, did make custom orders, or JJ acquired a license to produce their designs. One licensor was Jim K. Benton, who designed a line of simple face drawings, accompanied by current expressions. The line was called "Just Face It". The pieces were signed "J. Benton" with the copyright symbol and did not bear the JJ mark. JJ purchased a license from Mr. Benton to produce and sell his "Just Face It" designs in 1995.

Mr. Benton is a current graphic artist, who has won many awards, including awards for his Happy Bunny, Franny K. Stein and Dear Dumb Diary creations.

J. BENTON

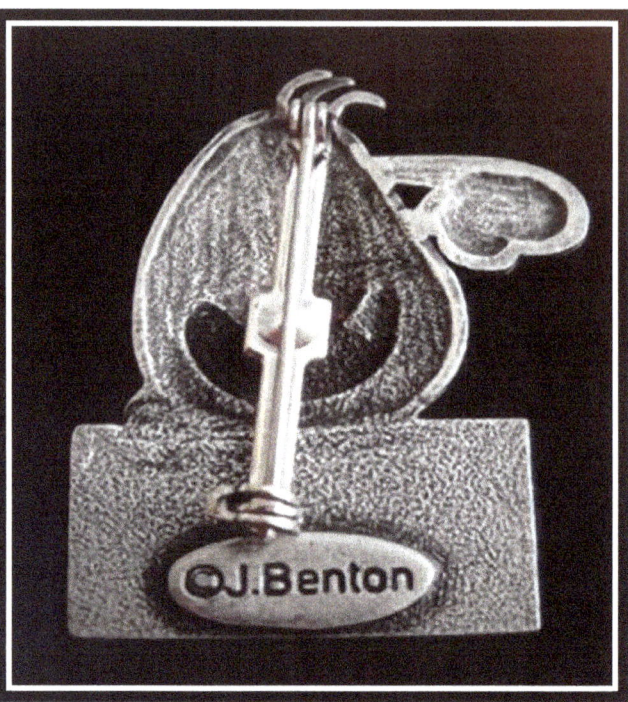

Jim Benton, artist; JJ manufacturer

SPOONTIQUES

JJ had a wonderful, mutually beneficial relationship with one of their major customers, Spoontiques. Spoontiques is based in Stoughton, Massachusetts. Spoontiques bought many items (mostly pins) from Jonette. Some were Jonette's original designs and included the JJ marking and some were Spoontiques original designs.

Ken Sawyer is the CEO of Spoontiques, and like Gordon, he went into business with his father, Hal Sawyer. Hal sadly passed away in 2004. Ken said they had a great relationship with Gordon, and his records show the relationship between the two companies continued from around 1994-2005. He said there was a period of time when the jewelry sold extremely well for Spoontiques. He noted that Jonette's designs were wonderful, and that the jewelry was made very well. Ken and Hal met Gordon at a jewelry show in Providence.

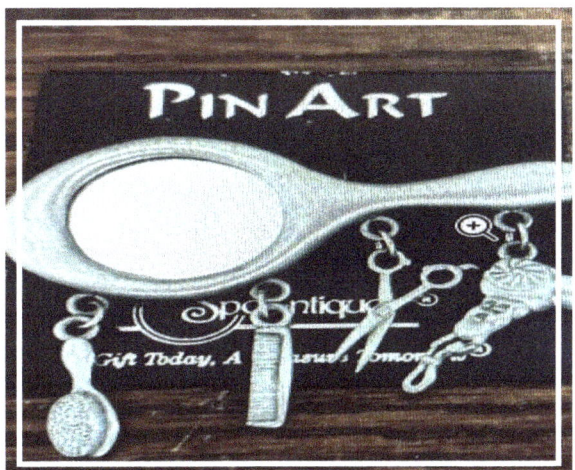

Spoontique examples online

Spoontiques originated in 1971, and remains in business to this day. They sell many giftware items including garden décor and drinkware.

MS. DEE

JJ also made pewter jewelry and trinket boxes for Ms. Dee. Ms. Dee was incorporated in 1974 in Mound, Minnesota and was headed by Ms. Deanne Moss. The "Ms. Dee" copyright was registered in 1982. It appears the items made for this company were all signed "Ms. Dee" or had an inventory number on them. They were not signed by Jonette. The Ms. Dee designs were clever, comprised of pewter trinket boxes that provided multiple pieces of jewelry. For example, a trinket box might have a pair of earrings incorporated into the top of the lid's design, with the pierced backs on the inside of the lid. The lid itself had a pin back, so it could be worn as a brooch. Inside, there might also be a necklace. The bottom of the box often had a saying inscribed, related to the theme of the trinket box.

Owl box with "WHOooo" inscribed inside, leaf earrings and the lid can be worn as a pin

In these pictures, you can see the detailed cat trinket box. The inside of the box has a pin back, so the cat lid can be worn as a brooch. The earrings are rhinestone studs, that serve as sunflower centers in the design on the top of the box. Inside, on the box bottom, is written "Meow" with a paw print. The box also contains a cat face necklace as well.

Ms. Dee also made a line of boxes with wooden bases and pewter lids, that were deeper than their feminine pewter boxes. This style was a men's line, where each lid had a tie tack incorporated into the lid design, instead of earrings. JJ made many of these boxes as well.

Example of Ms. Dee Men's line boxes with lids manufactured by JJ. The inside of the lid shows the back of the little sailboat tie tack.

Alan noted getting ready for the shows where Jonette would display its new lines and take orders was "crunch time." Sample boards for customer viewing were set up. New lines were displayed, along with popular older lines that were still in demand.

When Alan was asked, he noted some of his favorite creations were the animal and the Art Nouveau designs. He was particularly proud of the Art Nouveau pin he made based upon his wife's profile, as seen on pages 72 and 170.

After Jonette closed, Alan went to work for Bernardo Manufacturing in Rumford, Rhode Island. He worked there for eleven years, until he retired in 2020. Bernardo is still in operation today. Alan assisted the team of designers there by creating accurate designs and renderings using Adobe Illustrator software on his computer. Although he had been using Adobe Illustrator for ten years at Jonette, Bernardo gave him the opportunity to learn 3D software, and also how operate a CNC machine, which stands for computer numerically controlled. Once a line drawing was completed using Illustrator, the design was loaded into a 3D program where a "virtual" model would be created. The virtual model could be rotated on the screen to see it from all sides. Once finalized, the computer would then scan the surface of the virtual model and create a tool path to guide the cutting tool on the CNC machine, which would cut a precise and detailed model from a sheet of resin board. Even with all the technological advances, Bernardo still had, at least at the time Alan worked there, 3 or 4 model makers on staff. Alan's subsequent work for Bernardo gives us a chance to see how rapidly the jewelry manufacturing industry has changed due to technological advancements.

JANET PARKER PRATA
– freelance designer

Janet Parker Prata worked as a freelance designer for JJ for about six months in 1989, and then she went back and worked for the Company from approximately January of 1999 through the Company's closure in 2006. Most of her other freelance work was for companies that manufactured greeting cards and paper products.

Janet would come into the showroom and she and Gordon would discuss ideas. Gordon had many original design ideas, and would also have a stack of magazines where he would get inspiration from current trends. Sometimes he would do rough sketches of ideas he had-he was good at that. She described Gordon as a creative innovator and funny. She credits Gordon with all of the design ideas. After the design concepts were finalized, Janet would draw pencil sketches at her home studio, and then bring them back to Gordon for review and editing. She noted, "I learned a lot about what model makers had to do to create a 3-D model from a 2-D drawing. It was a learning curve for me. It took a while for me to understand the technical aspects of creating an accurate drawing for the model makers." Alan Weimer was a source of guidance for some of logistics of design for model makers, and she noted the model makers were true artists.

Janet described the JJ atmosphere as casual and relaxed. Gordon loved animals, which is why they were a frequent theme in the pins. He was friendly, and open to new ideas. She enjoyed working with him. Sometimes, Gordon would call in Alan to join their design discussions, whether it was to review mechanical design issues, or just to expand on a certain concept.

She noted that part of JJ's success was due to the humor in much of their jewelry, but that the Company also made many beautiful traditional designs. She recalls she created about 50% humorous designs, and about 50% traditional illustrations. She states the jewelry was of high quality, and that it is a credit to Gordon that the Company survived as long as it did. It was relatively small, compared to companies like Monet and Coro, but the Company survived much longer than others that failed when the overall industry started to decline in Providence.

STEVE VALLONE

Steve was JJ's longest term employee, working for Abe Lisker and then for Gordon. He started working for the Company around 1955. He was just 17 years old when he was interviewed by Abe for the position of delivery person. Steve knew nothing about the jewelry business when he interviewed for the position. The Company's packages had to be driven to the Post Office. The Company only had one car for transporting the packages, so sometimes, two or three trips to the Post Office had to be completed on a given day. As Steve said, "We didn't have UPS at that time." After about a 20 minute interview, Abe hired him on the spot. Steve recalls that there were only about 3 or 4 women working for JJ when he was first hired.

Steve did whatever work was needed to be done - he would pick up and deliver orders, sweep floors, help in the shipping department and also work in the factory, operating a drill press or foot press. He even picked up Abe's lunch on occasion- Abe always wanted an "American cheese sandwich with lots of mustard, and a coffee with three sugars". Steve worked long hours sometimes – 10-12 hours on a given day when business was hectic. When Abe was in charge, the business continued to use outside shops for much of the work-carding, wrapping, plating, etc. Steve would transport the product as needed. "I did whatever they needed; I didn't mind."

Steve had a wonderful rapport with Abe. They were always on a first name basis, and Steve said Abe "treated me like a son", and "I loved him dearly". After Steve was hired, he would be the first to get to the factory, which was located at 147 South Street, on the second floor. He would have to wait outside, however, until Abe's assistant, Marie, got to the office, to let Steve in. After a couple of weeks, Abe told Marie to get Steve his own key, so he could let himself in.

After Steve had been working for the Company ten months or so, the Company moved to 85 South Street, adjacent to Regal Plating Company. Business had grown, employees added, and they needed more space. Following the move, Abe asked Steve if he wanted to be in charge of shipping, which would involve supervising 18 women. Steve laughs about what a challenge that was at times! He was busy directing what needed to be sent out to be glued, painted, carded, etc., while still overseeing the shipping department. The Company did, however, get another fellow to take over deliveries.

The close relationship between Abe and Steve continued throughout his tenure at JJ. Abe and he went fishing, attended night baseball games, and Steve and his family were invited to Abe's summer home in Westerly. They often worked Saturday mornings, and Abe would quip, "You know, Steve, I'm Jewish. I shouldn't be working on Saturdays." Steve described Abe as a likeable, smart man, who was very honest. Ironically, when Abe showed Steve his yearbook, he was described in there as "Honest Abe." Abe liked to reminisce with Steve. Abe told him that when he was about 9 years old, his father took him to work with him. Steve thinks Abe's father may have had some connection with Lamson Oil Company, and the use of hooking tractor trailers with double loads for transport. This information, however, has not been verified. Abe's father wanted Abe to be a dentist, but Abe had other ideas.

When Steve was supervising shipping, Abe told him he didn't want to grow the Company any bigger than it already was. Steve indicated Abe liked to oversee everything, and wasn't comfortable delegating oversight to any significant degree. In contrast, Gordon was comfortable delegating and leaving others to get their jobs done, once he felt the others were competent, and operations were running smoothly.

Eventually, Abe was ready to slow down, and he wintered in Florida. He continued to go into the plant until shortly before his death at age 91. (Abe's wife, Geraldine (Jerry), lived to age 102!) Steve said JJ's operations really took off, and the Company realized tremendous growth after Gordon took over. Steve is also very fond of Gordon and his wife, Nancy, whom he describes as "wonderful people." He describes Gordon as a generous man, and more relaxed in the role of the Company CEO, compared to Abe. Gordon was willing to let others pull their share of the load and did not feel it was necessary to closely manage them.

When Gordon took over around 1972, the Company was employing less than 20 employees. Steven told a funny anecdote about a Christmas party at night, the first year after the Company had moved to Taunton Avenue. There was a band upstairs. Some of the men had too much to drink and rescue trucks were called. As Steven put it, "That was the last party at night."

Another great story Steven shared is how he met his wife. Right at the start of his career with JJ, at the ripe old age of 17, he had taken a delivery to Regal Plating. An Armenian woman, Bessie, worked there, and she asked Steven, "How would you like to meet a nice girl?" Being an able-bodied young man, of course Steven said "Sure", and out came his future wife, Annette, age 17. Steven and Annette shared 69 wonderful years of marriage, until her recent passing in 2023.

At the height of JJ's business, they were putting out at least 300 new items per year. Many competitors were looking at what JJ was coming out with each year. They used plastic cameos, rhinestones, onyx, and tiger eye in some of their creations. They did a line of alphabet pins and another line of Zodiac pins. They even made Y2K pins, when everyone was afraid computers would crash when we flipped centuries from 1999 to 2000.

Janet Parker Prata, designer

It wasn't just foreign competitors that were anxious to see JJ's new lines. Domestic competitors were also surveying the new products, and this eventually led to copyright infringement, as more fully detailed later on.

Steve recalled a mold maker who worked for JJ for 25 or 30 years, Johnny Martins, but he has passed away, and Nunzio Izzo, a JJ designer and model maker, who designed some of the mythological pins for which JJ is so well known.

Steven loved the Christmas lines JJ produced, recalling painted candles with red rhinestone flames, and wreaths.

Christmas pins from online pictures

HELEN NASUTA

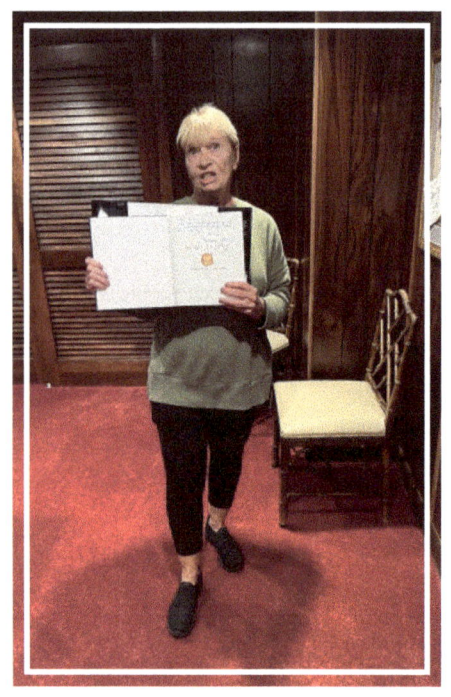

Helen served as vice-president of operations and worked for JJ for over 30 years. She noted high points of her time there included the feedback they would receive at the jewelry shows, when the new lines were introduced. Helen agreed with Alan Weimer that the greatest pressure was getting ready for the shows. She was instrumental in getting the jewelry sample boards put together. She also put together pricing sheets with the costs of different metals, stones, etc., which she would provide to Gordon so he could set the prices for each piece of jewelry. Gordon often would work until the early morning hours getting the prices finalized, as frequently, the new lines came together at the last minute.

Helen found Gordon to be a wonderful employer, honest and kind. She described him as very generous and that he helped everyone.

On occasion, Helen would travel with JJ's sales representative, Bruce McCowan, to Chicago or California, to show the company's sample boards, because the vendors couldn't come to the jewelry shows in Providence and New York. They even went to shows in Italy. The first two years, the shows went very well. The third year, in 1993, most of the JJ line was stolen. Helen and assistant Diane Santos, had to deal with the police and security guards in Italy. They ended up having to take a train to Switzerland and fly back home. That ended shows in Italy.

For the NYC and Providence shows, usually JJ's salesman Bruce McCowan would work one room, and Gordon would work the other, with them showing the same lines in their respective rooms. Many stores wanted to place their orders before other wholesalers came in. Customers over the years included Mervins, Amerimark, Dillards, Potpouri, Sears, Claire's Boutique, Steinmart and Marshalls. JJ jewelry was also found at Macys, BonTon, Dillards, JC Penny, Casual Corner, Accessory Lady and more, including party plans such as Avon and Park Lane.

In some cases, JJ manufactured pieces specifically and/or exclusively for customers such as Spoontique, Ms. Dee, Casual Corner and Park Lane. In those instances, the JJ copyright

Display from Italy show

might, or might not, be replaced by the customer's stamp. The number of employees grew to 125 and often two shifts were required to keep up with customer demand.

Helen was basically a jack-of-all-trades, checking factory orders, dealing directly with the customers and preparing for the shows. Once the Company started using computers, she would input the jewelry data in the computer. She also procured copyrights for much of the jewelry, including for items that were made in earlier years, but had not been copyrighted. She explained that initially the jewelry was dated on the pieces themselves, but once they started copyrighting their designs, they stopped dating the jewelry on each piece.

Helen received an interesting phone call one day-from the office of former Secretary of State Madeleine Albright. Ms. Albright was writing a book called "Read My Pins", as she had become well-known for sending discreet messages to world leaders by her choice of brooches. Ms. Albright wore JJ's gold spaceship brooch, with its three dangling aliens, to a meeting with Russian diplomats, to celebrate the U.S. and Russia space mission partnership. Ms. Albright's office wondered if Helen could locate another pin for the book. Ever resourceful, Helen did find another copy of the brooch and shipped it to Ms. Albright's office. Thereafter, Helen and Gordon received an inscribed copy of Ms. Albright's book, as a thank you for her assistance. (See more on Ms. Albright's book on page 74.)

The low point in Helen's career was when Gordon made the difficult decision to close the business. He was getting ready for retirement and was tired of foreign countries like Mexico, Japan, Korea, China and Taiwan copying JJ designs and charging much less than what JJ could charge with U.S. labor prices. He had no interest in moving manufacturing overseas with its child labor and unregulated working conditions. The Company had litigated copyright infringement cases, but they were costly and usually, the damage was already done. Gordon was also starting to experience the early signs of Lewy Body Dementia with parkinsonism. He at first thought he had had a stroke. He knew he was no longer himself and he no longer felt the drive to compete. Helen was the last employee left when the plant closed.

BRUCE McCOWAN.

Bruce McCowan was a full-time salesman for Jonette Jewelry, and also a salesman for the American Ring Company, a company that manufactured costume jewelry rings. Gordon recommended Bruce for the American Ring Company employment. Gordon was apparently comfortable with Bruce adding a second line to his sales work, since he was the one who recommended that American Ring hire Bruce.

Bruce went to school with Gordon, and based upon stories shared, the pair were quite mischievous in their younger days! Bruce stated "Gordon was good to me." At the time Bruce talked to Gordon about working for JJ, Gordon was trying to decide if he should hire a full time factory sales representative, or whether he should hire a contract sales representative, that might be selling lines from 3 or 4 other companies, in addition to JJ. In other words, he was evaluating whether a contract sales representative would be able to do JJ justice in marketing JJ lines, or whether it would be better to hire someone not otherwise obligated to sell for other companies, who could be taught about the industry, and be fully devoted to JJ products.

Bruce stated that when he started, "I knew nothing about jewelry. I worked as a shipper for a while, and started getting familiar with the industry. I started from scratch, and Gordon gave me that opportunity." He added, "I went on to work for him for 30 some years, and I got to know the industry only because of him."

Bruce described a shift in how sales were effectuated during his career. In the beginning, he only sold to wholesalers. If he had tried to call retailers directly, he would have been blackballed-it just wasn't done. Over time, the larger retailers such as Marmaxx (parent company of TJ Maxx and Marshalls) and Sears, exercised their financial clout, and expected salespeople to deal with them directly. As a result, many wholesaler positions were eliminated.

Bruce's work was varied. He would periodically call on wholesalers in the Midwest, and show the latest product lines. There were usually two large costume jewelry trade shows in Providence each year, and two smaller shows in New York City. He had a looseleaf book he made up with pictures of the merchandise. Some of lines ran for several years, as they retained popularity. He usually had a couple of sample cases too, displaying the actual pieces of jewelry.

The big change in the industry which ultimately led to the closure of JJ, and many other costume jewelry manufacturers in Providence, was foreign labor and competition. When factories started opening in China and other parts of Asia, American based companies could not compete with their cheaper, unregulated labor costs. The production of costume jewelry was very labor intensive, and American companies could not sell their products at the cheaper prices the foreign produced jewelry manufacturers were selling.

The decline in the industry happened over a shockingly short period of time. Bruce recalled that when he started, around 1973, there were pages and pages of jewelry manufacturers, finishers, job shops, assembly work companies, listed in the telephone book yellow pages. Providence was the logical place to start a jewelry business, because you could get everything done there- casting, plating, acquisition of materials, and the companies were comprised of a knowledgeable labor force. By 2006, at age 62, Gordon closed Jonette. He sold his creations and copyrights to a loyal customer and friend, Wally Karol from Chelsea International, in Toronto, Canada.

RAPHAEL LOPES

Raphael Lopes was one of JJ's model makers and he worked at the Company from 1987 or 1988 until it closed. He first worked for American Ring, doing assembly work. He went to JJ, because his father was working there. Initially, he worked in the tubbing room (dipping the jewelry) and swedging. He later moved on to the model making. Raphael said he liked everything about his work at JJ, and that "Gordon was the best."

Luckily for us, Raphael kept a small notebook of many of the designs for which he made models. Most of the following pictures from his notebook were made by Alan Weimer, but we have been able to identify some that were made by Janet Parker Prata. All the models were made by Raphael.

Designs by A. Weimer, except octopus, designed by J. Parker Prata. Models by R. Lopes.

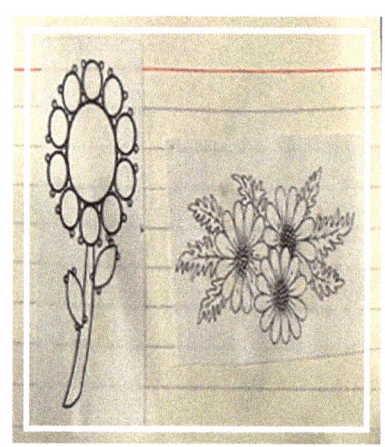
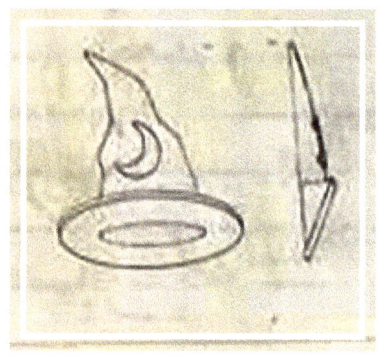
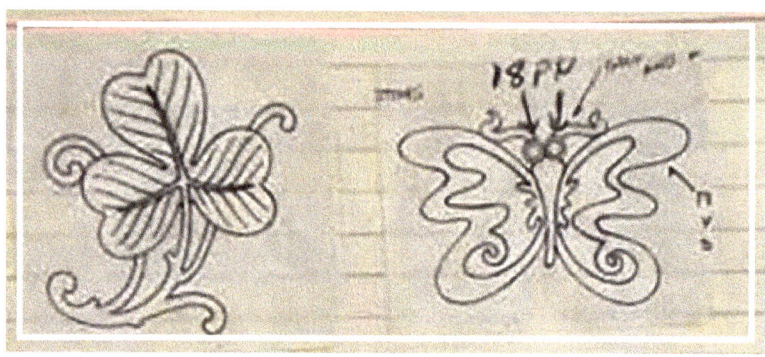

Designs by A. Weimer, except the cat with mouse, dog and butterfly, designed by J. Parker Prata. Models by R. Lopes.

Designs by A. Weimer, except the nursing pins, designed by J. Parker Prata. Models by R. Lopes.

Designs by A. Weimer, except the bird with flower, nurses always care, 2 little girls looking at sun, hand with heart, #1 Friend dog house and small nurse, designed by J. Parker Prata. Models by R. Lopes.

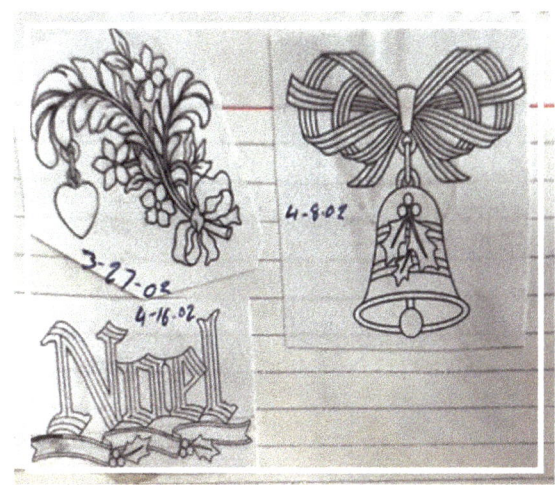

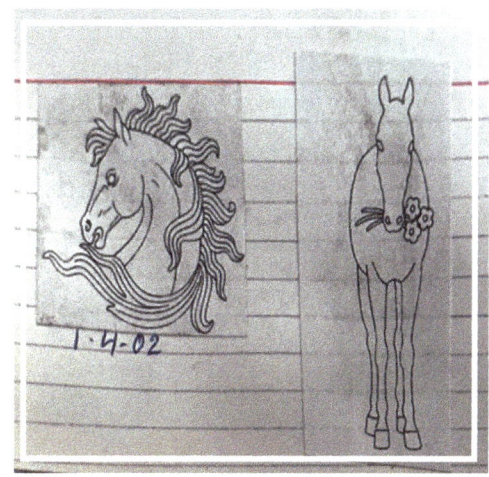

Designs by A. Weimer, except the "eat veggies", nativity, "happily ever after", horses and fish face, designed by J. Parker Prata. Models by R. Lopes."

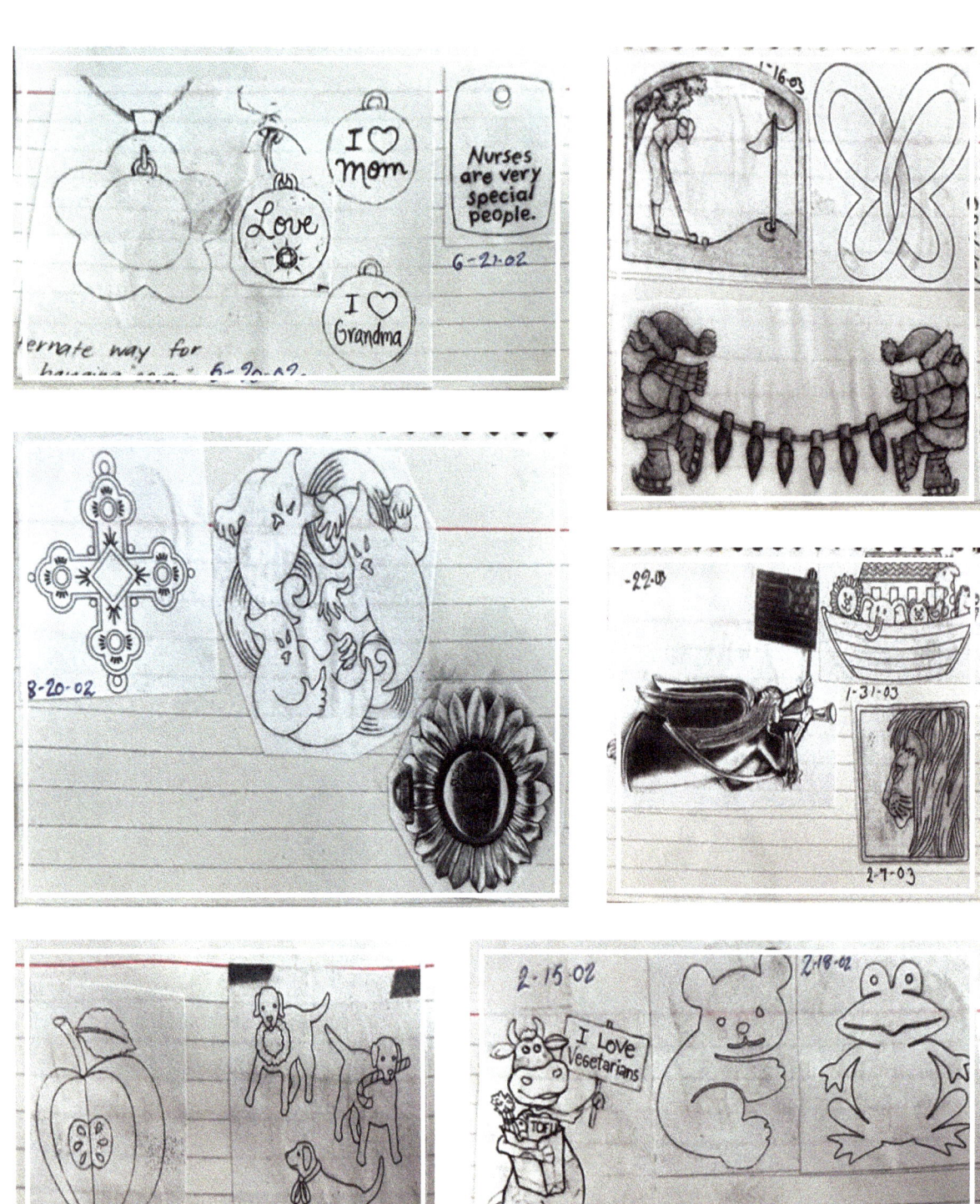

Designs by A. Weimer, except the Love, Golfer, Santas with string of lights, "I love vegetarians", designed by J. Parker Prata. Models by R. Lopes."

Designs by A. Weimer, except the basket with bird, Christmas trees, "The Way to my Heart", "Kick Meat", flying geese pins, designed by J. Parker Prata. Models by R. Lopes."

DIANE SANTOS

Diane's story at JJ is a wonderful example of how opportunities can blossom in unexpected ways. Starting out as a receptionist/bookkeeper, her dedication and talent led her to explore inside sales, and eventually, the exciting world of outside sales.

One memorable experience involved a trip to the Italy show with Helen Nasuta. When the entire line was stolen, they ended up leaving Milan early by train. The scenic ride was a silver lining to a challenging situation. "As bad as that was for the Company, it gave me an opportunity to see the beautiful Swiss Alps".

Like many at JJ, Diane thrived on the company culture. She loved the people, the energy, and the chance to travel the world! Starting at a young age (around 19 or 20), Diane soon found herself exploring Miami, New York City, and even Milan. She noted, "I loved the people, the characters...I was young, and I got to travel!" These trips were undoubtedly formative experiences for a young woman launching her career.

She fondly remembers attending shows with Bruce, even sleeping in the room filled with beautiful jewelry displays! The popularity of JJ was evident in the lines that formed outside showrooms at locations like the Biltmore and Holiday Inn in Providence, and even at trade shows in New York City. Diane noted, "Vendors were eager to partner with JJ due to the company's reputation for exceptional quality and unique designs."

JJ display for one of the Italy shows

Diane describes Gordon as extremely approachable and experienced, "the Liskers are a wonderful family." Abe, in particular, left a lasting impression by sharing stories, both joyful and poignant. Diane's 13-year tenure at JJ, spanning roughly from 1985 to 1998, is a testament to the positive and enriching experience she had during her time there.

THE EARLY DAYS AFTER GORDON TOOK OVER

Steve Vallone

Left to right, Jim Dumachelle, Alan Weimer, Helen Nasuta

Helen Nasuta, interpreter, Diane Santos at an Italy Show

Helen Nasuta

Helen Nasuta, her assistant (not a JJ employee) and Judy, JJ's bookkeeper

II. A HAPPY REUNION

Despite limitations imposed upon Gordon due to Lewy Body dementia, he clearly enjoyed seeing all of his colleagues when we gathered at Gordon's home to review the history of JJ. He got quite a kick out of hearing Bruce McCowan's "war stories" from their high school and college days, which were highly entertaining.

THE COMRADERIE AMONGST THE JJ CREW IS ALIVE AND WELL!

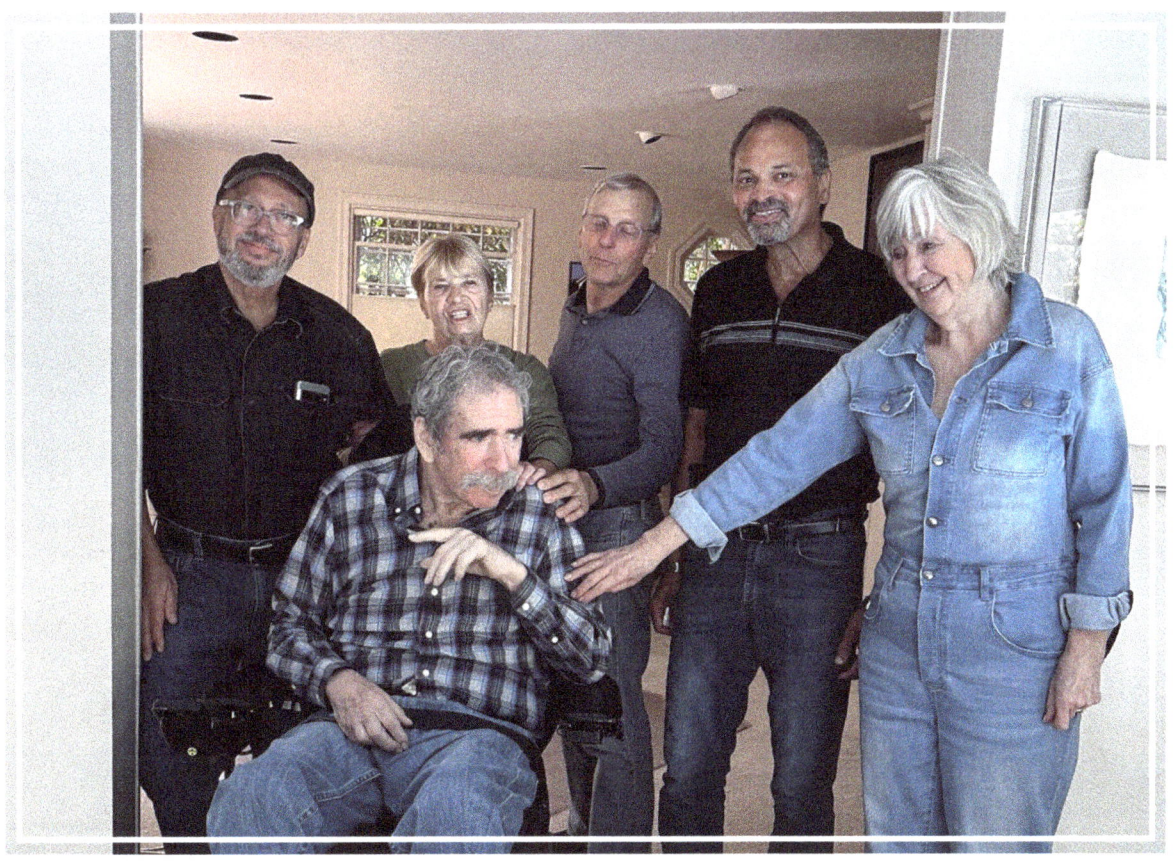

Alan Weimer, Helen Nasuta, Bruce McCowan, Raphael Lopes, Nancy Rozendal, Gordon Lisker (seated).
October, 2023

III. THE MANUFACTURING PROCESS

The process would usually start with an idea from Gordon, but there were also ideas from both the in-house and the independent contractor designers. The designers would then take Gordon's ideas and bring them to artistic life. The overall process was design approval, model making and sculpting, mold[1] making, casting and then vibing, to take off any rough edges. After that, finishes would be applied and any additional treatments, such as beads, crystals, etc., as well as adding the pin backs or chains.

One of the designers would give a model maker an accurate line drawing of the next creation. When Alan Weimer made his designs, he really didn't have to add much color or shading, because the model makers were right there, and he could give them verbal direction. Alan was especially impressed with the work of the late model maker, James Dumachelle, who worked for Jonette for almost 40 years. Alan always knew James could execute even the most complicated of models.

At the top of this picture: A vulcanizing machine with a mold frame containing a round rubber mold with models inside.

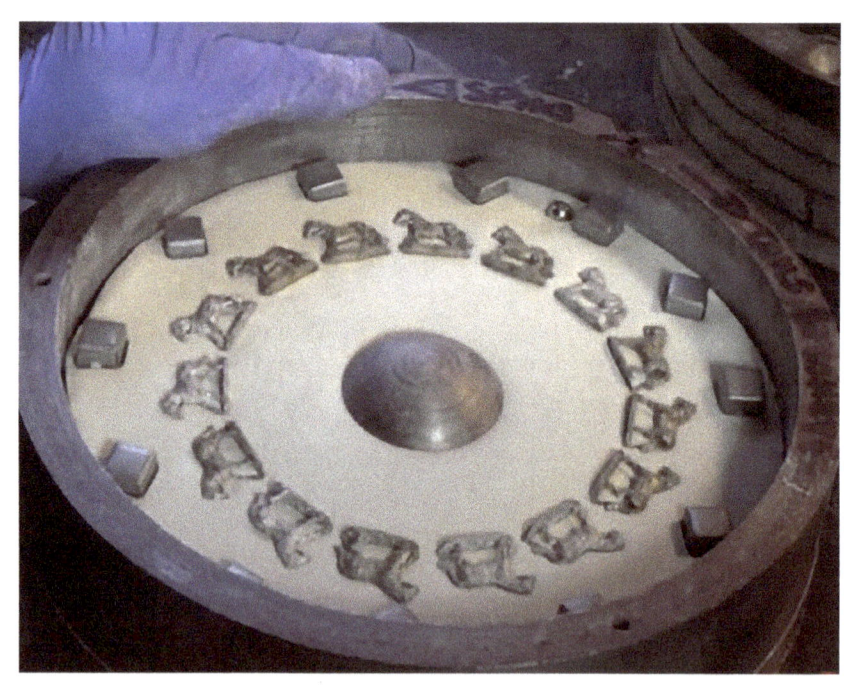

mold in frame

The model maker would use a piece of tin flatstock varying from 1 mm to 7 or 8 mm thick, depending on the amount of relief a piece might require. The design was glued onto the flatstock,

---

1   A mold is made by arranging models on a round piece of raw rubber, (which is soft and pliable) into a steel frame. It is covered with another piece of round, uncooked rubber and a flat steel cover on top of that.

PAGE 46

and then the model maker would cut out the outlines of the design, using a jeweler's saw. Once cut out, the sculpting of the piece would proceed, using files and a small hand held drill with various rotary cutting tools attached. Some model makers like to carve the metal with flat gravers, which are like miniature chisels with wooden handles, that fit into the palm of one's hand. Model makers used their gravers in the same way a sculptor uses chisels to carve wood. Tin is a relatively soft metal that carves beautifully. The models would then be put into molds.

vucanizer

The top of a model maker's bench is shown below, showing a design that has been glued onto a piece of flat stock. The design is ready to be sawed out, carved and shaped into an original

At bottom: A steel mold frame and lid. The frame is heated from the top and bottom. Pressure is applied by pumping up the red bottle jack. Initially, the rubber is soft and is squeezed to confirm to every detail of the models. When the mold has cooked and cooled, the two halves are opened, the models removed, and channels are cut so that molten tin can flow into the mold cavities.

casting machine

After the rubber has cooled, it is hard, but flexible, similar to the consistency of a car tire. The finished mold is placed into a casting machine and a cover is put over the mold.

The lid is closed and the mold inside begins spinning rapidly. As the molten tin is poured through a funnel and into a hole in the top of the mold, centrifugal force moves the metal into the empty cavities.

Once cool a knife was used to remove gate marks and then vibed to remove rough edges. This preceded all finishing touches.

Gordon created an archival system of hinged wooden design boards where a sample of every model was attached with its number. The models could then be matched with the stored rubber molds should the Company wish to remake pieces with or without modifications years later. All original models were all kept in a huge safe.

About a dozen were cast in each production mold, and usually a couple of dozen were made for each run. JJ carried out every step of the manufacturing process at the factory, with the exception of electroplating, which they sent out to be done.

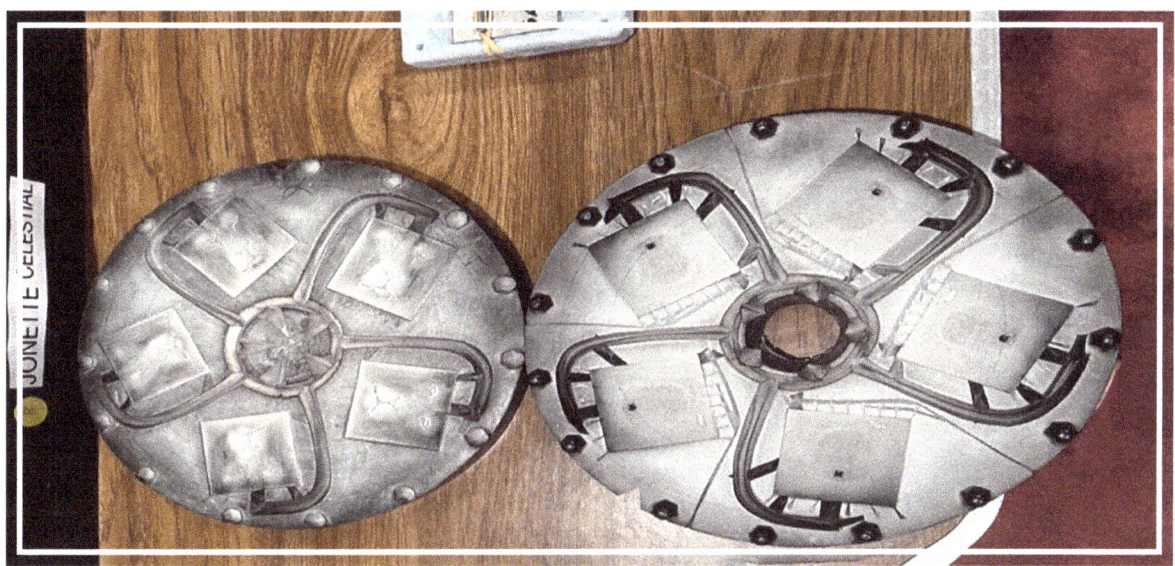

Picture of lion face pin molds. This pin was a popular item.

Pewter was a natural finish that could be applied in-house. The raw castings would be dipped into a mild acid solution that oxidized and blackened the surface. A finishing wheel was then dressed with a gritty polishing compound, and the castings were "brushed" with the wheel until most of the blacking was gone. This would give the piece the classic brushed satin finish, with black remaining in the crevices and engraved lines to help give the item contrast and definition. The pieces were then sprayed with a clear lacquer to protect the surface and prevent re-oxidation of the metal. The oxidized brass finish is similar to the pewter, except that brass is an electroplated color. The oxidizing, brushing and lacquering were applied in the same manner as the pewter.

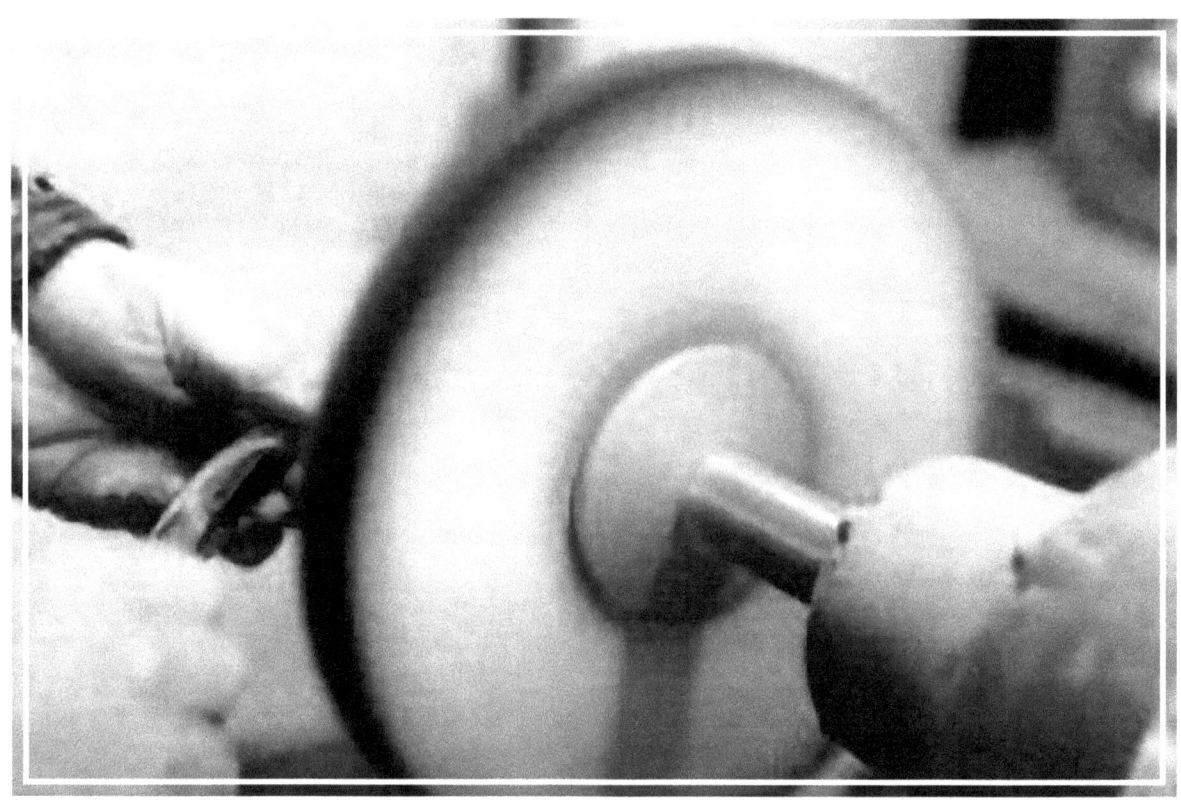

A finishing wheel

The Company used a swedging tool to attach pin backs to the castings. First, a form to hold the pieces was made from the same material used to make dental molds. The pin castings had a square post on the back where the pin back findings were placed. A drill press with a piece of drill rod (slightly hollowed out on the end) would spin and press the square post until it mushroomed over, holding the pin back tightly in place.

If stones were needed, they were glued on. If items were not going to be pewtered, they were simply "tubbed" in the vibe room to clean them, then swedged or joints and catches were added. Once completed, the items were inspected, carded, placed in "cardboard beer tray" bins and were then ready for packaging and shipping.

Pin Finding

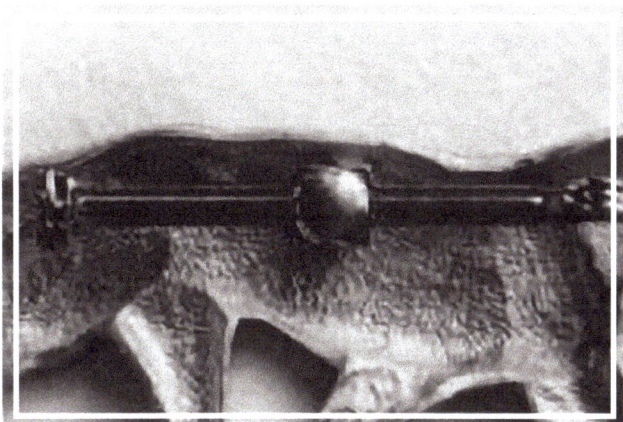

Square Post *Swedged Pin*

Advancements in the jewelry manufacturing included JJ's design for the pins that had doors that could be opened, and there would be a scene inside that was partially or completely hidden when the door was closed. Gordon designed the tiny hinge, that had to be custom fabricated. In-house designer, Alan Weimer, noted that the opening door concept could not be "knocked off" for some time, because manufacturers couldn't figure out how to recreate the hinge! Another JJ innovation was the design that allowed dangles on the pieces to be incorporated into the mold, so the dangles didn't have to be added separately.

Online Photos

The plant on Taunton Avenue was basically two floors. The employees would come in the side door. The front door opened into the showroom and offices. Beyond that was the factory, where mold making, casting, adding beads and linking would occur. Upstairs was the design and model making space, and the pewter room. The Company used a link-a-matic machine for the linking. There was some hand painting, gluing, pearl setting and sample making. The wrapping, labeling and shipping was done upstairs, and then the packages were sent downstairs on a conveyer belt. They could put up to 40 packages on the belt at a time. Orders were usually shipped out.

The amount of jewelry made was dependent upon the orders the Company received directly from customers, mostly through its salespersons.

IV. CURRENT PRICING

Look at sites like Ebay and Etsy to get a feel for the prices of JJ jewelry. There is quite a range of prices-some pieces are being offered in the $8-$12 range, and others run up as high as $130. Most are being offered in the $15-$35 range on the internet sites. You can often find individual pins for less at thrift stores or consignment shops. You should see "new" if the pins being sold are being made by a company other than JJ. Also, if the Seller is offering you the ability to buy more than one pin, it is often (but not always) a sign that the pin is of recent vintage. If the new copies are being made from the original JJ molds, they should still be as charming as ever. Be aware, however, that as noted throughout this book, many foreign and domestic companies made knockoffs of JJ creations, during and after JJ's tenure, so those pins will not have the same detail or charm as the original JJ creations.

Sometimes buyers can get better prices if the JJ jewelry is being offered in a lot. The good news is that because JJ made so many creations, there is still plenty of opportunity for collectors to acquire pieces at affordable prices. The bad news is that some pieces have become very collectible and their prices have soared. Some examples garnering higher prices include the alien pins, the mechanical (opening door) pins, the art deco and art nouveau pieces, the mythical creations and the ones that reflect JJ humor, as depicted throughout this book.

V. ADVERTISING

JJ mostly marketed its products through its salesman, Bruce, and the trade shows in Providence and NYC. Thus, there is very little printed material. Fortunately, Nancy had one brochure that is shown here, along with an example of Gordon's business card, and Alan Weimer's current business card. Isn't that Art Deco business card holder JJ made wonderful? The brochure is great, as it illustrates a partial view of the variety of products JJ made. You will see picture frame and locket pins, bookmarks, perfume bottles and letter openers. The brochure is undated, but we believe it is from the mid-nineties.

Alan Weimer, designer; Jim Dumachelle, model maker

All the perfume bottles were designed by Alan Weimer; bookmarks designer, unknown.

All the perfume bottles were designed by Alan Weimer; bookmarks designer, unknown.

All these bottles designed by Alan Weimer

PAGE 57

Alan Weimer designed the dimensional sled pin

These letter openers were all designed by Alan Weimer. The letter openers are rare, and very seldom seen on the secondary market such as Ebay or Etsy.

School house pin was designed by Alan Weimer. It has a tiny brass bell linked onto the pin.

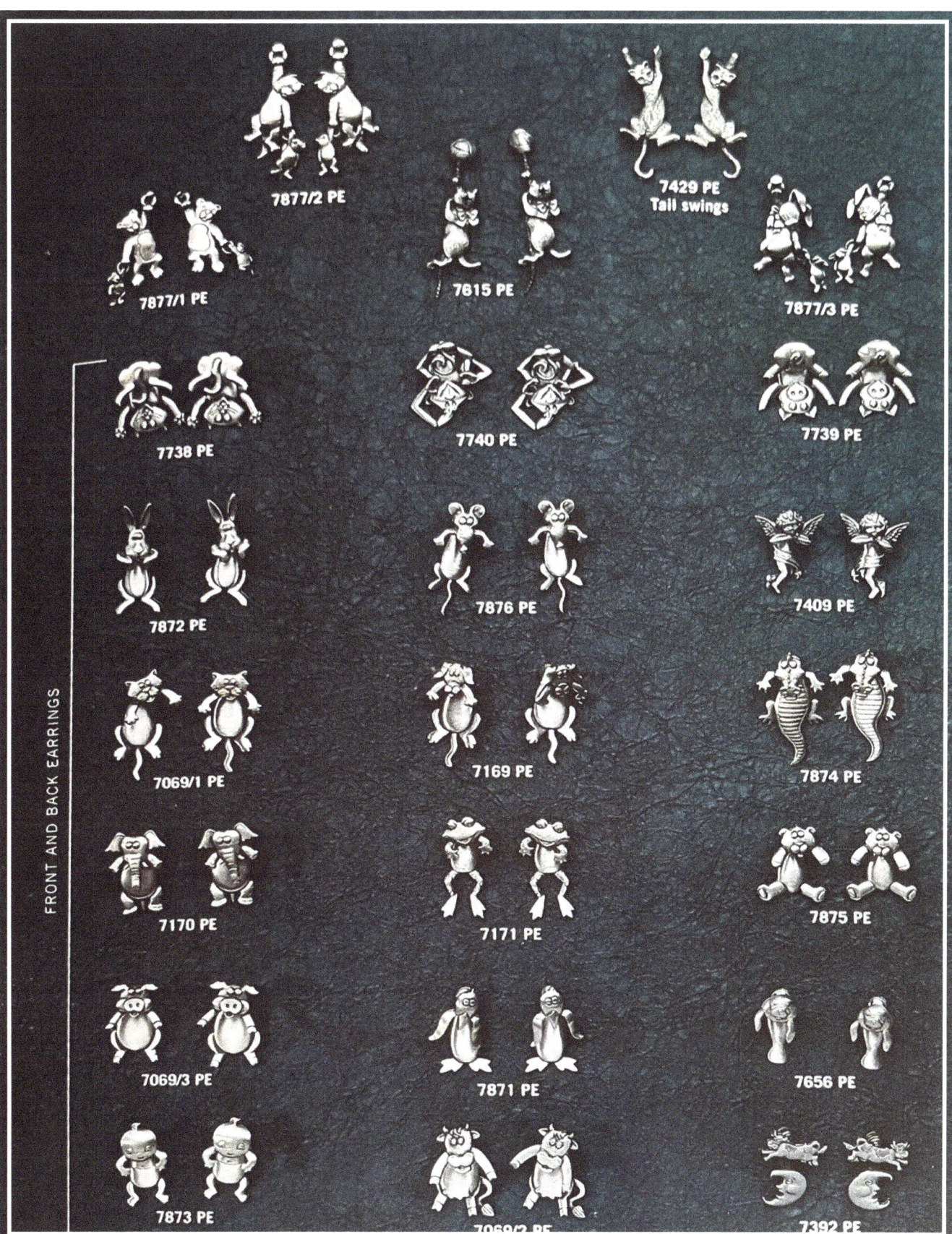

PAGE 69

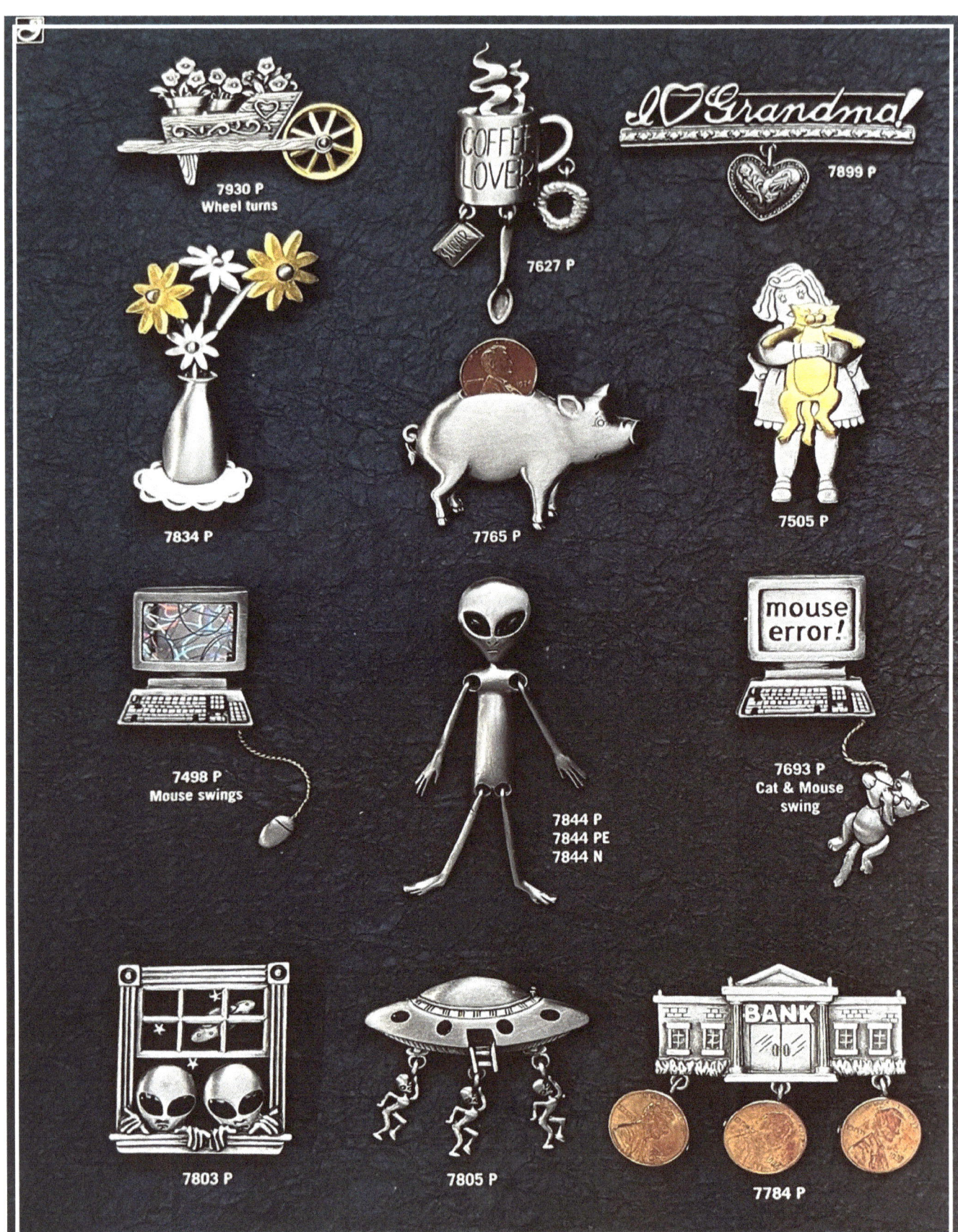

PAGE 70

Another item that JJ made was standing picture frames. They are miniature works of art! These were all designed by Alan Weimer and the model maker was James Dumachelle.

Standing mirror and picture frames

Sun mirror

VI. VARIETY OF DESIGN THEMES

JJ produced so much jewelry, that there is hardly a trend the Company didn't cover. The sheer breadth of the designs is staggering. Many examples of the jewelry are found in this book, but we couldn't possibly show them all to you, or you would never be able to lift it off the table! Holidays were popular – Christmas trees, angels, wreaths, candles, etc.; Valentine's Day, Easter, Mother's Day, 4th of July, Halloween and even Columbus Day, to name a few. Animals of every kind, from domestic, such as cats, dogs, pigs and cows, to wild ones, from tigers, lions, bears and wolves. Professions were highlighted as well, from teachers, to nurses, to real estate salespersons. The nursing profession jewelry sold very well after 9/11, and undoubtedly, saw another resurgence on the secondary market, such as Ebay and Etsy, after the Covid pandemic. JJ also had a whole southwestern line, "Santa Fe" featuring coyotes, landscapes and cactus. JJ also made some very elegant pins, as depicted below. Yet it is the whimsy and humor that is frequently mentioned by jewelry experts in highlighting why JJ creations remain so collectible today.

One of Alan Weimer's favorite pieces is this elegant Art Nouveau brooch based on a profile of his wife.

A line drawing showing the humor that is seen in many of Alan's creations.

An example of how design inspiration could come from anywhere, Gordon saw a life size sculpture of a metal horse in the lobby of a Florence, Italy hotel. That was then translated into JJ's "ribbon" and "wire" animal figures.

Another example of design inspiration followed a visit by Gordon, Nancy and another couple for "a back tour" of Zoo New England in Boston, Massachusetts, conducted by the Zoo veterinarian, Dr. Hayley Murphy. The couples were given strict instructions as they walked into the back of the gorilla exhibit, including 1) walk single file 2) stay against the wall behind a line a few feet away from the bars (because the gorillas have long strong arms!) and 3) under no circumstances, make eye contact with the gorillas, as their reaction is to throw poop! Unfortunately, one person forgot the last rule, and the group got spattered! The gorillas loved company and one sobbed uncontrollably as they were leaving. One of the gorillas was named "Little Joe". Gordon asked Hayley for a photo of him and he asked

Alan Weimer to design a depiction of him for a pin(March, 1997). Jim Dumachelle made the model. The pin was produced in pewter, brass and gold.

Gordon was on the Board of Directors of the Roger Williams Park Zoo in the late 1990s. In 1997, "Paul", a tree kangaroo came to the Zoo from the Metro Zoo in Miami. A conservationist and animal behaviorist, Dr. Lisa Dabek, was employed by the Zoo. A fundraiser was held to help cover her travel expenses to study the tree kangaroo in its native habitats of Papua New Guinea and Australia. JJ manufactured tree kangaroo pins to be sent to those who donated, and they were also distributed to the individuals Dr. Dabek interacted with during her research visits.

Gorilla pin based on Little Joe 1997 Designer Alan Weimer, model maker Jim Dumachelle

Tree Kangaroo, Alan Weimer, designer, Jim Dumachelle, model maker, 1998

VII. LEGAL ISSUES

As mentioned previously, there were copyright infringement lawsuits. Manufacturers copied from one another frequently, and sometimes customers took JJ ideas and brought them to other jewelry manufacturers, in search of a better price. Under Gordon's direction, JJ was one of the first companies to start copyright infringement litigation. One lawsuit was based on the design of the pin depicting a cat looking at himself in a mirror, which was a popular seller for JJ. (That pin was so popular, the retired employees still remembered the item number, "Number 5423".) In the Vintage Fashion and Costume Jewelry article[1], the Liskers explained the design infringement difficulties: "In the 1980s, their hand-painted enamel line was very popular, and sales were very strong. Eventually, their pieces were copied in Taiwan. Within six weeks, after Jonette had a show and shipped samples out, the whole line was coming in from Taiwan, including displays with the JJ mark casted on the back in most cases. JJ's new line was wiped out. Gordon was called upon to start new lines, and again, Taiwan, Korea and other people jumped in and began copying." The article went on to say, "Gordon, at that point, in a defensive move, started copyrighting designs. He registered the copyrights and prosecuted the offenders, thus establishing a strong reputation for a willingness to fight to protect JJ's copyright."

In addition to the headaches of copyright infringement lawsuits against foreign and domestic entities copying JJ designs, JJ was threatened by a lawsuit from Jim Henson of the Muppets. Henson requested that JJ cease and desist the manufacture and distribution of pins which Henson alleged depicted "Miss Piggy" and "Kermit the Frog". JJ, of course, had always humanized animal depictions in its jewelry, but one customer, Rosecraft, Inc., asked Jonette to make pins that more closely resembled the Muppet characters. Ultimately, the case was settled out of court, and Jonette and Rosecraft shared the Offer of Judgment expenses. All models, molds and pieces were destroyed.

JJ started using the Artifacts trademark in 1986, with 1986 written in Roman numerals at the bottom. As the Artifacts design originator, Alan Weimer, stated, "In retrospect…we were inadvertently making a record of what was occurring in popular culture at a particular moment in time…Artifacts, if you will." Some of JJ's smaller customers needed a card provided for each piece, and the label also served as an additional copyright protection. The Artifacts label was another way of verifying authentic pieces of JJ jewelry, distinguishing them from the "knockoffs" being produced in the U.S. and foreign countries. Alan came up

---

1   Vintage Fashion and Costume Jewelry, Volume 8, #3, Summer, 1998, Lucille Tempesta, Publisher

with the name, thinking the pins memorialized current trends, and would represent items of cultural or historical interest long after they were produced.

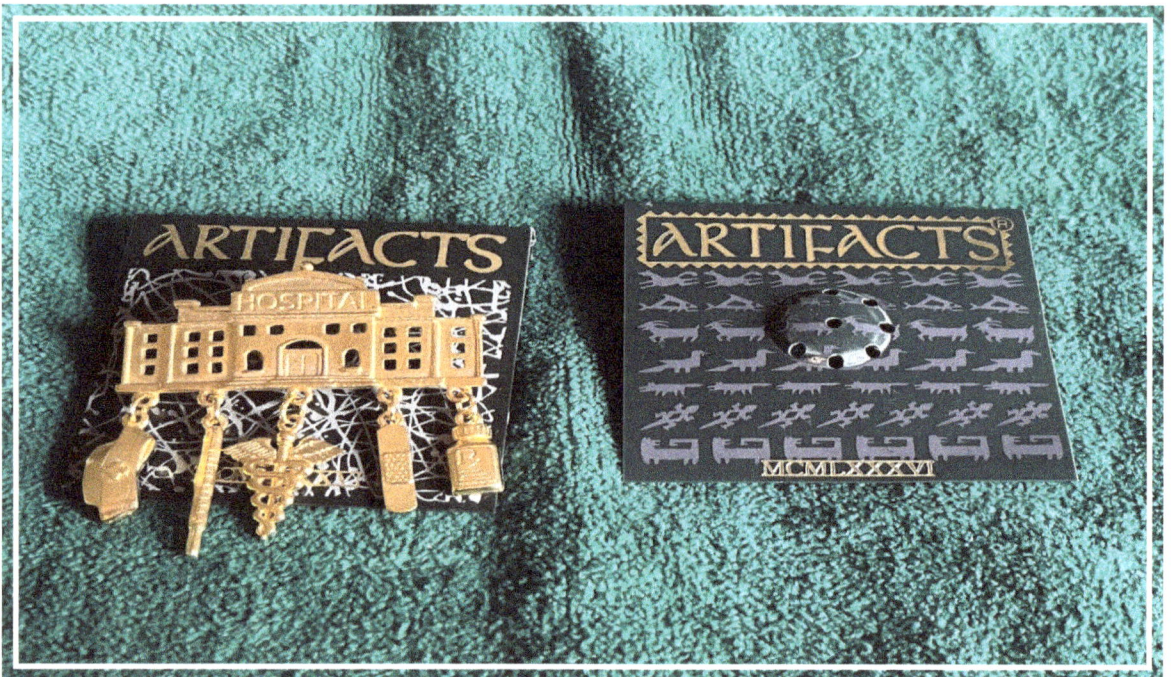

VIII. JJ'S CLAIM TO FAME - RECOGNITION OF JJ'S ARTISTRY BY JEWELRY PROFESSIONALS AND CELEBRITIES

Danielle Oliva Tefft, jewelry writer and GIA accredited jewelry professional, noted in her blog, "If you like vintage figural jewelry, you most probably have come across wonderful figural pieces with the "JJ" mark..." and that "Figural jewelry popularity exploded in large part due to companies like Jonette"[1]. In the Kaleidoscope Effect, the author states, "Widely known to collectors, JJ Jewelry conquered all due to its distinctive designs. Besides, they are easily recognizable. This is not just a decoration, but a work of art. JJ vintage ornaments grow in value every year, and therefore are a great investment."[2] In Warman's "Costume Jewelry Figurals Identification and Price Guide" by Kathy Flood, Ms. Flood states "Vintage J.J. pins are bargain gems, some are beautiful creations, full of surprises. Modern designs are witty, and the product of active imaginations."[3] Anne Mitchell Pitman highlighted a horse pin made by JJ, and noted, "J.J. Jewelry is quite popular, because they made something for everyone."[4]

Celebrities enjoy JJ pins too. Former Secretary of State Madeleine Albright wore many pins, choosing jewelry themes fit for the occasion she was attending. She chose JJ's spaceship pin, with its dangling aliens, to celebrate the U.S. partnership with Russia in the skies, and it was given a full page picture in her book, "Read My Pins". In her book, Ms. Albright noted that her use of pins to send a small message in her diplomatic role, was purposeful, and that "The world has had its share of power ties; the time seemed right for the mute eloquence of pins with attitude."[5]

---

1 6 10/20/2019 "Found in the Jewelry Box Blog" by Danielle Oliva Tefft, Jewelry writer, "The JJ Mark Stands For Jonette Jewelry Company."

2 Kaleidoscope Effect, "Jonette Jewelry Co-JJ vintage Jewellery," nasvete.com

3 8 Warman's Costume Jewelry Figurals, Identification and Price Guide by Kathy Flood, Krause Publications, 2007, page 9

4 "Inside the Jewelry Box, Volume 3" by Ann Mitchell Pitman, page 149, Collector Books, a Division of Schroeder Publishing Co., Inc.

5 10 "Read my Pins-Stories From a Diplomat's Jewel Box" by Madeleine Albright and others, Melcher Media, 2009, pages 110,

The actress Colleen Dewhurst, who played Murphy Brown's mother (1989-1990) wore a gold tone fashion pin made by JJ and the model, Hazel Moor, was photographed in Time Magazine, February, 1990, wearing the elegant set of earrings and brooch, depicting a sleek gold tone panther cat lounging over a black oval.

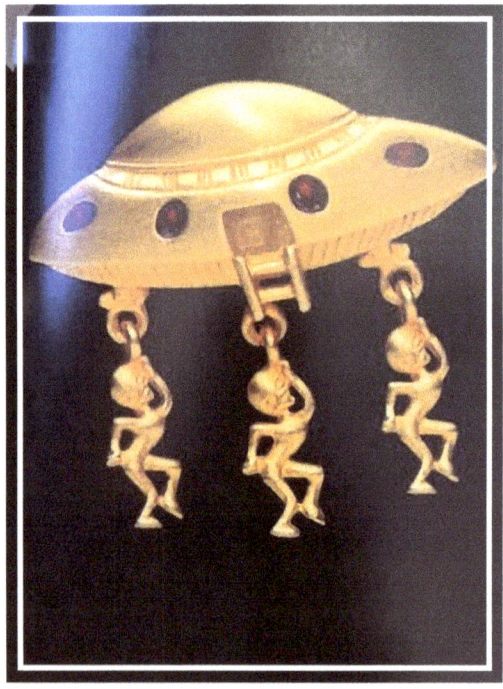

Actress Hazel Moor, 1990

IX. PROVIDENCE, RHODE ISLAND - THE JEWELRY DISTRICT

The Jewelry District is a neighborhood of Providence, southeast of downtown, that was the center of jewelry manufacturing beginning in the nineteenth century. Within the District is the Providence Jewelry Manufacturing Historic District, which was added to the National Register of Historic Places in 1985 and expanded in 2012.

By 1880, Rhode Island's jewelry industry accounted for more than one quarter of the nation's jewelry production. During its heyday, large costume jewelry manufacturers abounded, from large companies like Coro, Trifari, Monet, Swank and Speidel, as well as smaller companies. The industry peaked in 1978 with 32,500 workers. Thus, the location of the Providence Jewelry Company, and its successor, the Jonette Jewelry Company, in Providence, was a natural fit.

Unfortunately, a rapid decline in American costume jewelry manufacturing occurred. As previously noted, there were 32,500 workers in 1978[1], and there were 900 Providence jewelry firms producing 80% of the industry's costume jewelry in 1986[2]. By 1996, the number of jewelry workers had shrunk to 13,500[3].

---

1   Wikipedia, The Free Encyclopedia, Jewelry District(Providence), en.wikipedia.org/wiki/Jewelry_District_(Providence).

2   https://estatesintime.com/2018/09/01/jewelry-capital/"Rhode Island, Jewelry Capital of the World and How it all Happened" by Bruce Barnwell

3   Wikipedia, The Free Encyclopedia, Jewelry District(Providence), en.wikipedia.org/wiki/Jewelry_District_(Providence).

X. RECOGNIZING PROVIDENCE'S RICH JEWELRY HERITAGE – THE PROVIDENCE JEWELRY MUSEUM

JJ's rich heritage is shared by many other jewelry manufacturers that existed during Providence's heyday as the Jewelry Capital of the World. As part of the celebration of that heritage, Peter DiCristofaro, has helped found the Providence Jewelry Museum. Peter is a pharmacist by occupation, but his family manufactured and designed jewelry. His knowledge of the industry is amazing. Within the Museum walls was a wonderful, huge display of JJ cat pins, both domestic and wild. It was worth a visit to see the JJ collection, as well as the other fine examples of jewelry on display. Eventually, the bulk of the Lisker's remaining inventory of JJ items will be housed in the Museum.

The Museum was temporarily located in the Technic Campus, 1 Spectacle Street, Cranston, R.I. The Museum is in the process of fundraising, with the goal of raising enough funds to acquire and renovate the Arnold-Palmer House, one of the oldest buildings in Providence. "Iron"ically, the home has nothing to do with the golfer! It was built by a flour trader, Daniel Arnold, in the 1830s. Arnold then sold the home to Joseph Palmer in the 1850s, who later manufactured gold rings at his firm, Palmer and Capron.

One of the particularly exciting concepts the Museum proposes to incorporate into the new location, is a re-created jewelry manufacturing factory floor, where visitors can make a piece of jewelry, using authentic, historic machinery. Much more information regarding the Museum can be found at the Museum website: www.providencejewelrymuseum.org While the process of jewelry manufacturing has changed due to rapidly evolving computer technology, preserving the history of the remarkably creative jewelry manufacturers of the past, such as JJ, is important. As Peter Cristofaro said, "Providence made little works of art".

Peter DiCristofaro

Part of the 15 foot display of the JJ cat collection formerly on display at the temporary Museum.

XI. DATING JONETTE JEWELRY

Unfortunately, it is hard to find dates for all the JJ jewelry, particularly from the 1950s through the early 1970s. When Steve Vallone, long term employee of JJ, was asked, "How do you date the early JJ jewelry, when Abe ran the Company?", and his answer was, "You can't! He said at one time, they kept all the discontinued pieces in one place, but that inventory is long gone. Since the pieces weren't signed, nor copyrighted, it would be very hard to know if any early piece is indeed a JJ creation.

During the late 80s, the pieces were actually dated on the back. When the Company started copyrighting their designs, it stopped dating the jewelry on the pieces themselves. Then, they marked the jewelry with a stylized JJ on a raised cartouche. While looking up copyright dates could be helpful for the pieces that were copyrighted contemporaneously with production, there were many pieces sent in for copyright protection long after the date of production. Still, this book can provide guidance on dating for a large number of pieces. In addition, many pieces can be dated generally by decades of production, based upon content.

The early 70s was a period of great interest in space. In 1972, Apollo 17 landed on the moon. Skylab became the first U.S. space station in 1973. Apollo and the Russian Soyuz docked in orbit in 1975 and "Star Wars" was released in 1977.

The mid to late 70s also marked the end of the Vietnam War, the Bicentennial, the debut of home computers and the crash of American Airlines Flight 191, killing 271 people. Thus, patriotic, military, aircraft and computer themes were incorporated into JJ designs during this time. Also, In the late 70s and early 80s, there was a surge of nostalgia for the 50s. In the 80s, there was interest in the mystical realm, such as dragons and wizards, celestial themes, etc., that continued through the 90s. Art Deco and Art Nouveau themes were always popular.

In the mid-eighties, the AIDS epidemic was on the minds of everyone. Nurses were being recognized for their life saving endeavors, and JJ made a huge inventory of brooches praising their efforts. The world was becoming more aware of environmental concerns and preservation of endangered species. JJ's designs of tigers, bald eagles, leopards, gorillas, lions, snow leopards, elephants, sea turtles and even butterflies reflected the interest of so many to ensure their preservation. The famous Willie Nelson/John Mellencamp Farm Aid concert occurred during this time as well, and JJ produced popular pieces depicting farm animals, such as pigs, cows and horses, and farm related equipment like tractors.

Phantom of the Opera and Star Wars were huge hits. The space shuttles Columbia and Discovery were launched, and the Challenger exploded, all of which inspired Gordon and his designers. Men's jewelry became popular in the mid to late 80s, and the Jonette men's chains and bracelets were sold to Pierre Cardin as part of his men's line.

Janet Parker Prata, designer

Harry Potter was popular from 1997-2001, giving JJ an opportunity to issue mystical and celestial lines. Steven Spielberg's Jurassic Park, inspired dinosaur creations.

After the tragedy of 9/11, when the Twin Towers in NYC were taken down by terrorists, killing many innocent people, the U.S. was focused on patriotism, grief, and ultimately, peace and hope. Pins with patriotic and angel themes were popular.

Luckily, the Liskers saved many of the artist renderings of the pins, which bore dates, so some specific dating will be found in this book. Additional dates were found in copyright list records.

Lion

XII. THE BIG SELLERS

Helen Nasuta and Bruce McCowan identified some of the popular sellers – the celestial pieces, sixties type flower pins from back when Abe ran the company, Halloween, the horse with flowers in his mouth, all the nursing related pins, many of the Christmas pins, including the Noel, dove and the "9006", nativity scene brooch, the Egyptian cat "bookends" pin, etc.

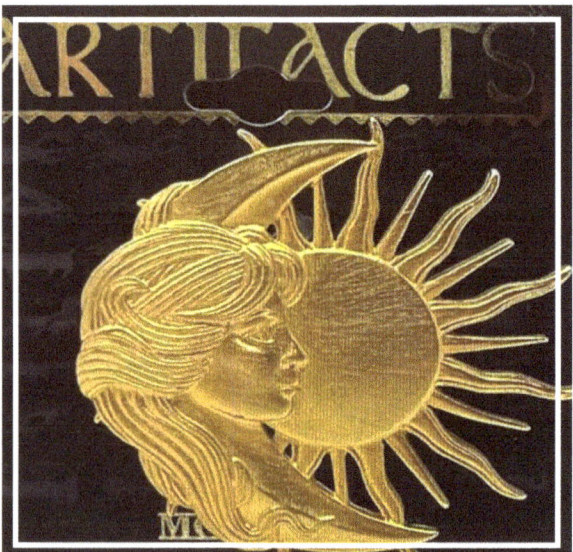

These two celestial pins were designed by Alan Weimer

Online pictures

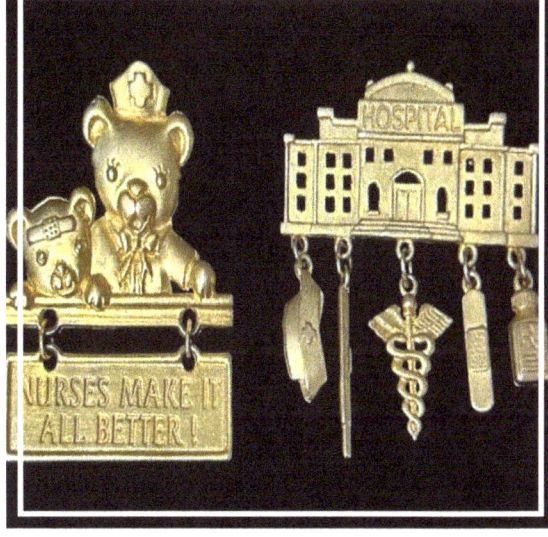

Horse with Flower in his Mouth   *Online Pictures*

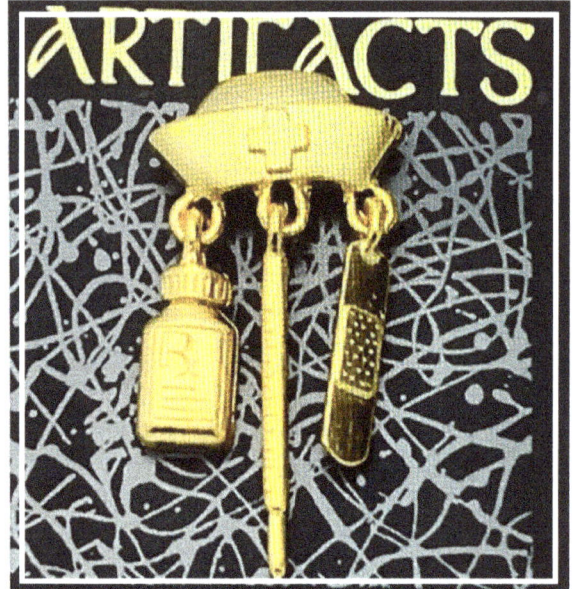

Egyptian cat "bookend" brooch designed by Alan Weimer

The volume of orders was based on show orders. Gordon had it down to a science, and 90-95% of the molds made ended up going into production. Unfortunately, David Lisker would have been one of the best sources of production numbers, and he is no longer with us. Although Helen Nasuta couldn't state the volume of production, she stated she would run reports, and they were sequenced according to popularity. She noted some pieces were hard to "let go", or stop production, because they had been so wildly popular. It is believed JJ made at least 100,000 items per year.

Wally Karol, who purchased the remainder of the Company, has a few pieces in limited production now. Seville Casting is making them for him. Their feel might be a little different than those made by JJ, but the designs themselves are from the original molds, so will look the same.

XIII. HUMOR IN DESIGN

Gordon was well known for his sense of humor, and he approved incorporating humor into many of the pieces the Company manufactured. Fantasy scenes were also used, and the humorous and fantasy themed pins remain extremely popular to this day. In this lot, Row 1, a pewter crescent moon looks terrified to see a flying cow jumping over it. In the next, a big mouthed alligator with pointed teeth salivates as he prepares to bite into a human sandwich. Row 2: A dangling long legged moose looks quite pleased with himself. Next to the happy moose is a cow that apparently got stuck trying to jump over the moon. The last pin in Row 2 shows a dog shutting a refrigerator door on a shocked cat. Row 3: Talk about a computer bug! A big beetle with large teeth takes a bite(or should we say byte?) out of a computer. A classic science fiction movie comes to life in the next pin, when a flying dragon dwarfs a city skyline. JJ made variations of this brooch, replacing the dragon with a flying pig, a pterodactyl and a hovering flying saucer. In the next scene, flirting coyote earrings are especially charming, due to their facial expressions. Last row, an example of one of JJ's moving parts pins. A brass google-eyed alligator has a mouth that opens, and when it is open, a small bird inside his jaws is revealed.

Bug eating computer, designer Janet Parker Prata

XIV. EXAMPLES OF JJ CREATIONS WITH SOME ARTIST RENDERINGS

There is such a staggering breadth of designs, that we decided to just put the examples of JJ products in a rather random fashion, and then allow the reader to look up a specific item by category index. We tried to cover a broad range, but we were constantly coming across new designs during our research.

JJ is well known for its mystical creations, from dragons breathing fire to wizards holding crystal balls. The fine detail in these images shows the talent and creativity of the JJ artists, model makers and mold makers. These pictures are from JJ's records.

The three designs above are by Alan Weimer

PAGE 91

Designer Alan Weimer *Designer Nunzio Izzo*

Designer Alan Weimer *Designer Alan Weimer of Pegasus above*

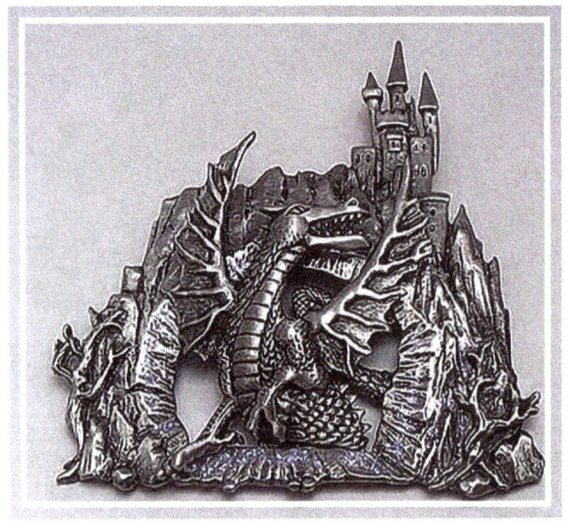

Designer Alan Weimer *Designer Alan Weimer*

Designer Ginny Stevens   *Designer Alan Weimer*

trio tack pins

Designer Alan Weimer   *Designer, Alan Weimer of castle above*

mystical charm bracelet

Designer Alan Weimer   *Designer Alan Weimer*

Designer Nunzio Izzo

Designer Alan Weimer

The two designs above are by Alan Weimer

Co-author Nancy Rozendal has assembled most of the remaining stock she and Gordon retained after JJ closed. She has organized them in display cases, with the intent to donate them to the Providence Jewelry Museum. The following pictures illustrate the wide array of designs that were imagined by Gordon Lisker, depicted by JJ's in-house and independent contractor designers, and actualized by the Company's model and mold makers. It was their magical collaboration that made JJ such an enduring, successful company.

Real estate, funny chefs, banks and more

Butterflies and Insects

This is where all the flowers have gone!

Sweet 16 pins, large key, small nursing pins, Janet Parker Prata, designer

A little birdie told me...

Egyptian Themes and More

Most of the nursing pins in the second row were designed by Janet Parker Prata

Wild animals on the loose!

Unicorns pewter and gold finishes

Mythological and Historic

PAGE 99

The breadth of JJ Designs is certainly exhibited here

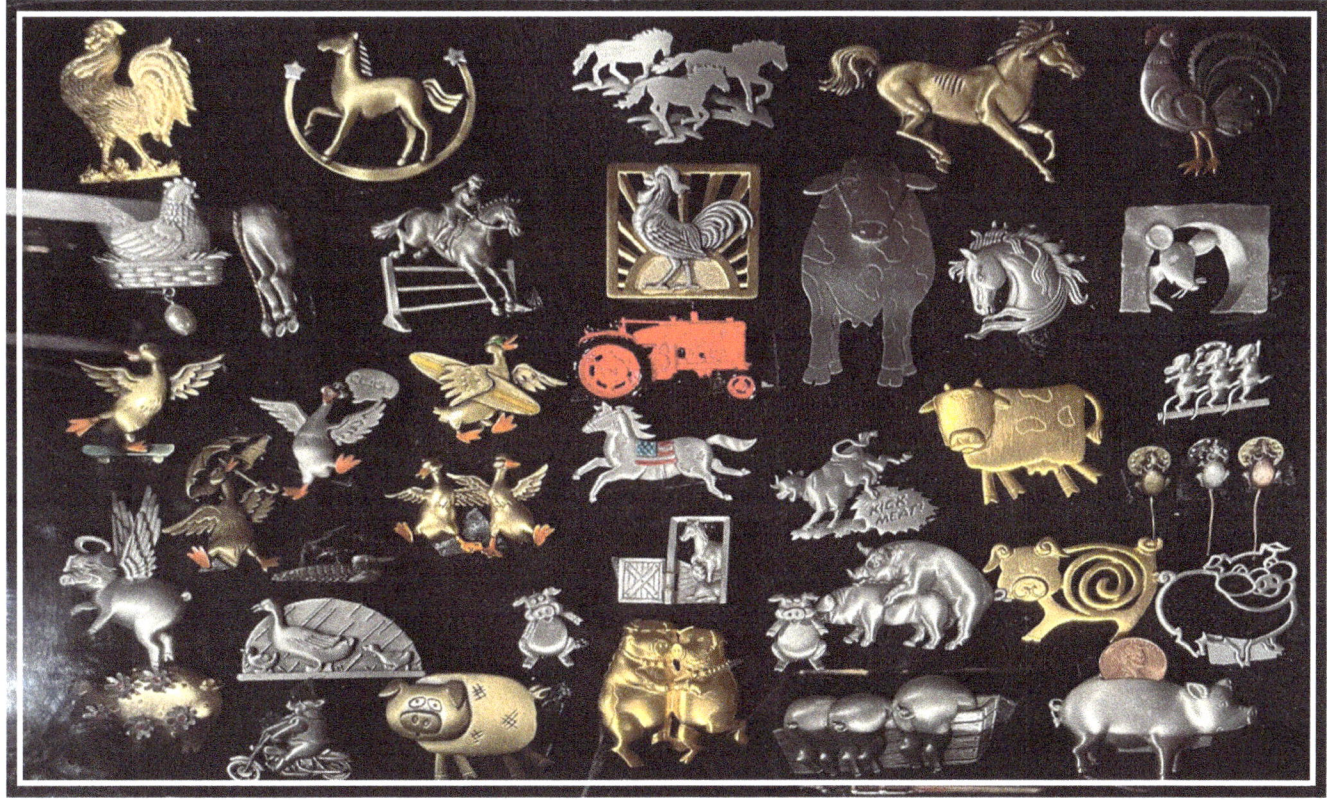

Top row, running horse, designer, Janet Parker Prata

Pewter cross with greens stones, gold center stone, designer, Janet Parker Prata

A little bit of everything

Frog in bathtub reading book, frog with pink flowers and the seek New Horizons pins, designer, Janet Parker Prata

PAGE 103

Angel with wings, chef with wine glass, and chef opening lid off fish, designer, Janet Parker Prata

Moon saturn swirls

One of the wonderful elements of preserving JJ's history is the found in the Liskers' retention of many of the artist's illustrations that led to the final product. In the following pictures, you will see examples of the artist's rendering, next to the finished pin. In the first picture, we see a zebra on paper, that is turned into a bronze patina brooch. The bunny on the next page is so realistic, that I think I can see his nose twitch!

Zebra, 1989

Bunny, designer Janet Parker Prata, 2002

Hippo and moose, Janet Parker Prata, designer

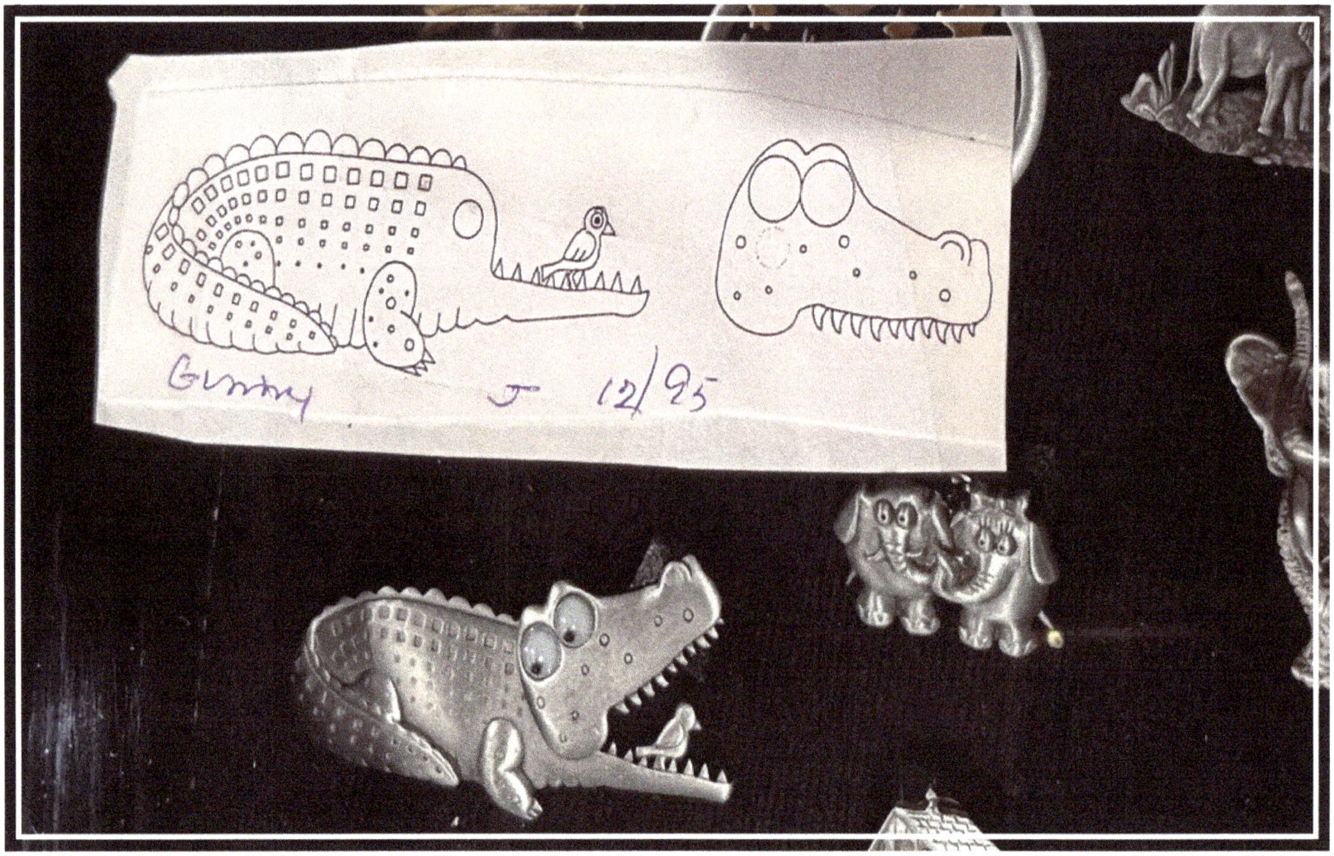

Mechanical alligator, Ginny Stevens, designer, 1995

Beaver, Janet Parker Prata, designer, Jim Dumachelle, model maker, 2003

Monkey, Alan Weimer, designer, 1998

Rocking Horse, Janet Parker Prata, designer; Keith Curvelo, model maker, 2005

Pigs Pigging Out! Alan Weimer, designer; Jim Dumachelle, model maker, 2003

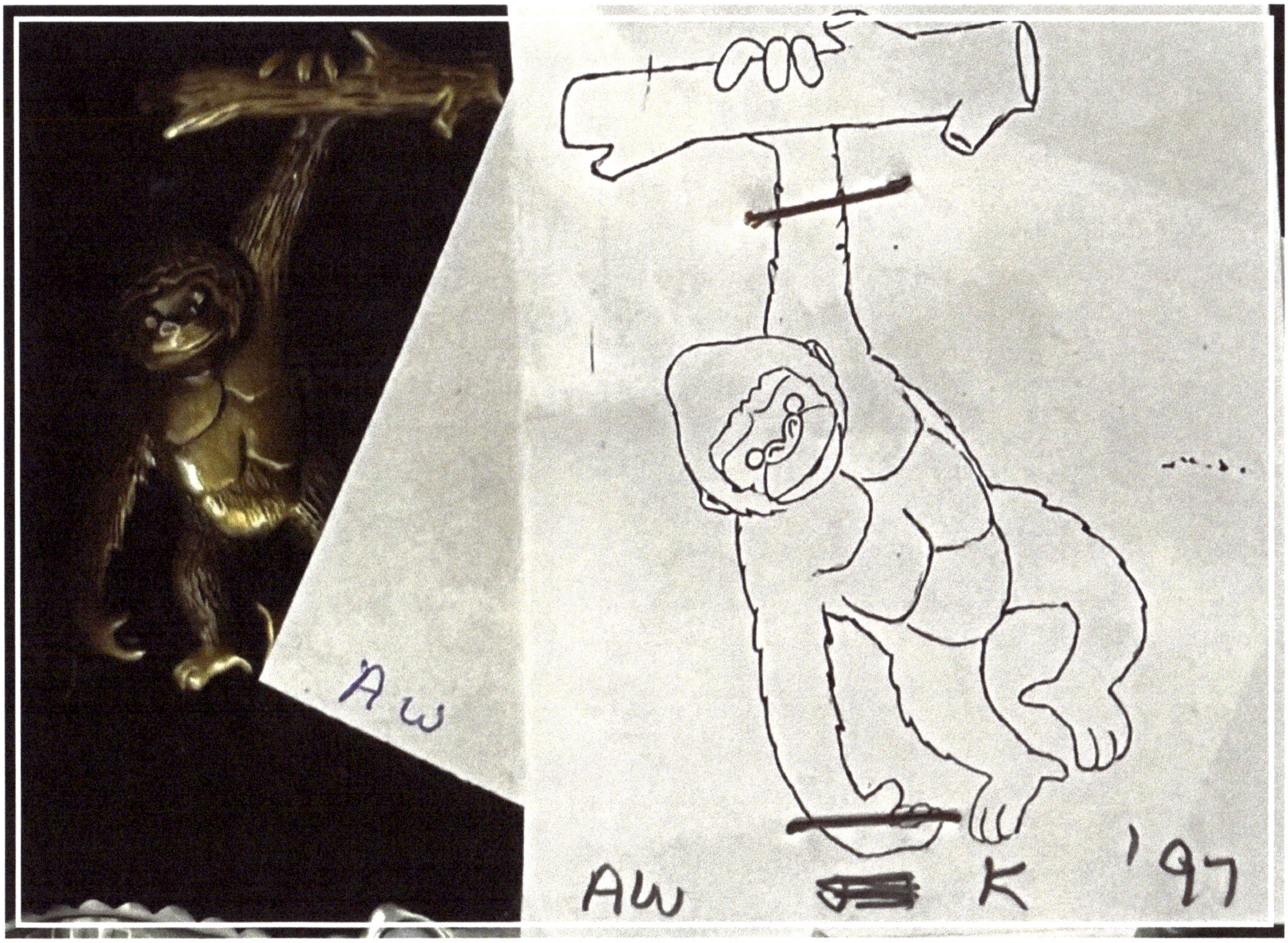

Consumers went ape over this brooch Alan Weimer, designer, 1997

Designer, Janet Parker Prata

Surf's Up, Janet Parker Prata, designer, Keith Curvelo, model maker, 2005

Wolves Alan Weimer, designer, 1996

Flower Pig, Janet Parker Prata, designer; Keith Curvelo, model maker, 2004

Rooster at Sunrise, Alan Weimer, designer; Keith Curvelo, model maker, 2004

Tractor, Alan Weimer, designer, 1997

3 Dancing Mice Janet Parker Prata, designer, Tony Martins, model maker

Rhinestone hearts and swirl brooches, designer, Janet Parker Prata

Makin' Bacon, JJ humor coming through; designer, Nunzio Izzo,

Piggy bank, Ginny Stevens, designer, Eric Bergeran, model maker, 1996

Designer, Janet Parker Prata

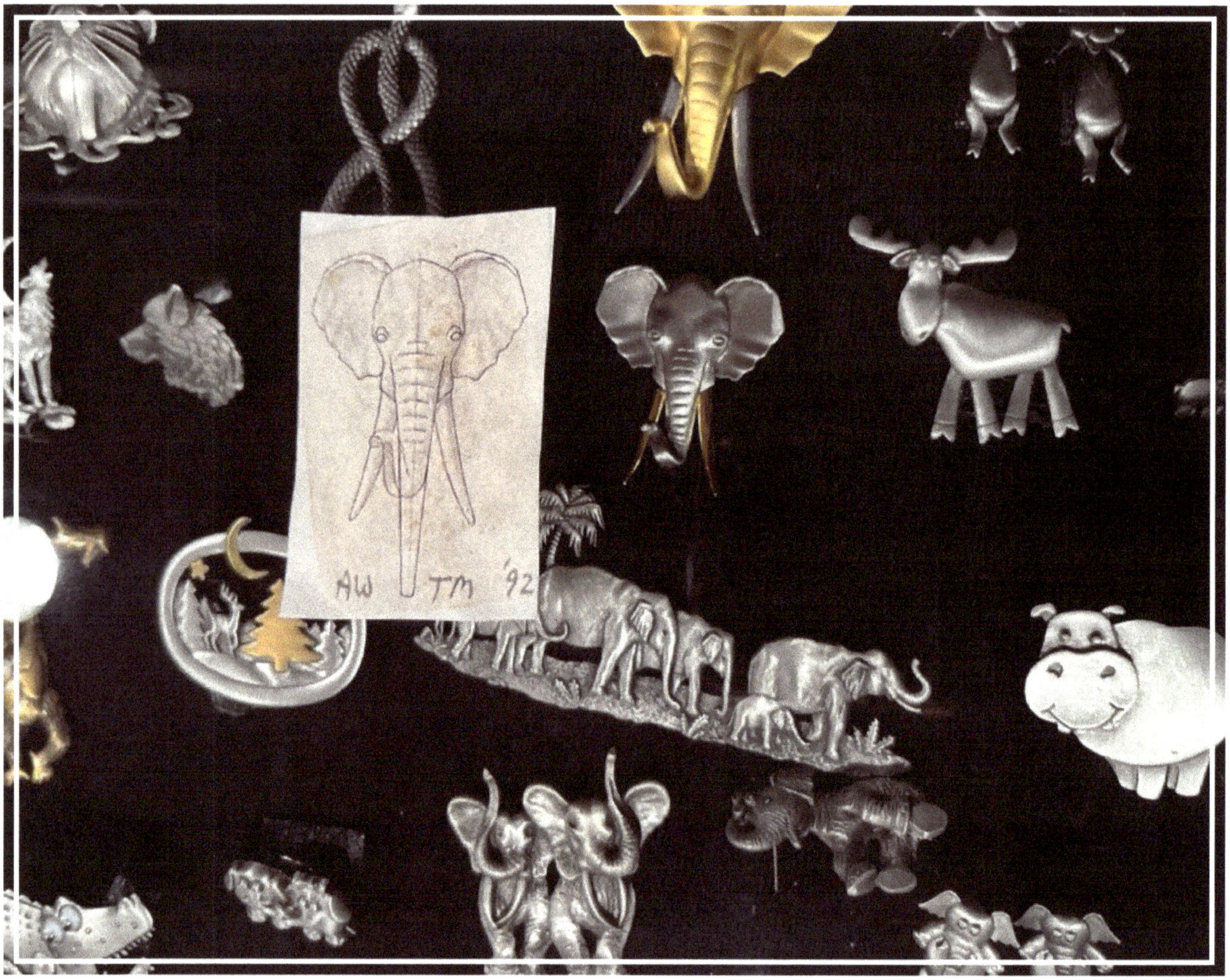

Elephant, Alan Weimer, designer, 1992

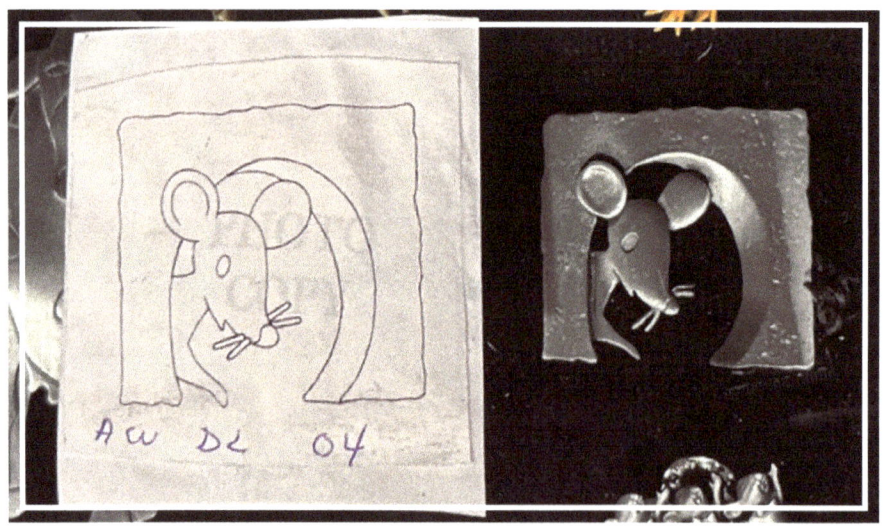

Alan Weimer, designer, David Lisker, model maker, 2004

Free form designs

Alan Weimer, designer, David Lisker, model maker, 1992

The above sketches were by Janet Parker Prata

Art Deco business card holder

Alan Weimer, Virginia Stevens, designers, David Lisker, Model Maker 1997

Nunzio Izzo, designer, not clear on model maker, 1992.

Alan Weimer, designer, Jim Dumachelle, model maker, 2002

Alan Weimer, designer, David Lisker, model maker, 2003

Alan Weimer, designer, Keith Curvelo, model maker, 1998

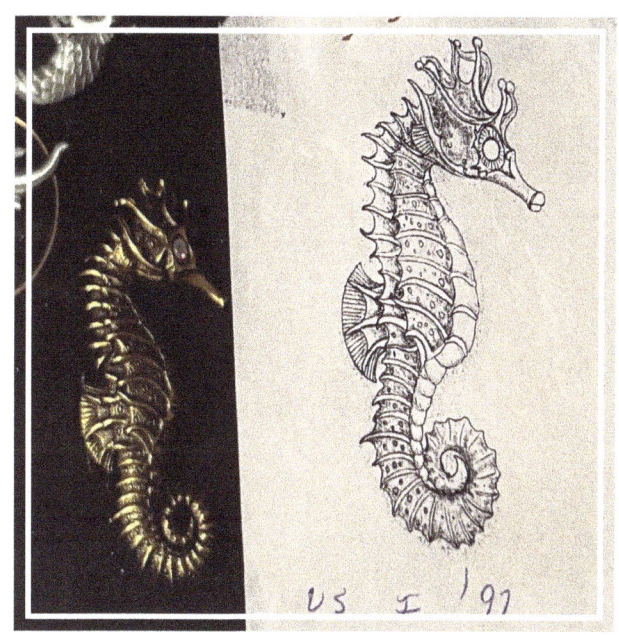
Virginia Stevens, designer, Isaac Newar, model maker, 1997

PAGE 121

Virginia Stevens, designer, David Lisker, model maker 1997

Alan Weimer, designer, April, 1997

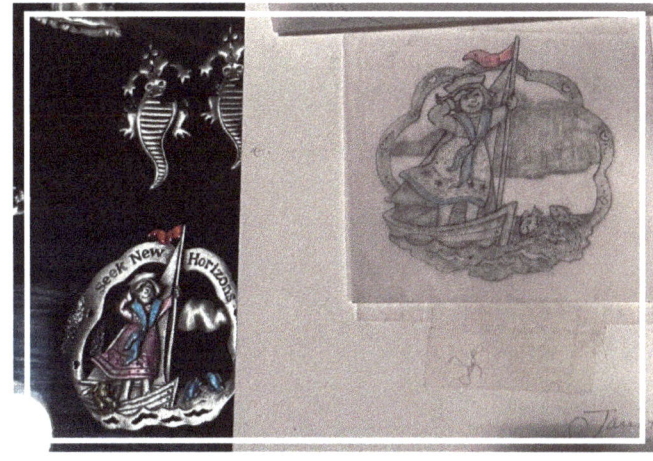

Janet Parker Prata, designer

Alan Weimer, designer, Raphael Lopes, model maker 1995

PAGE 123

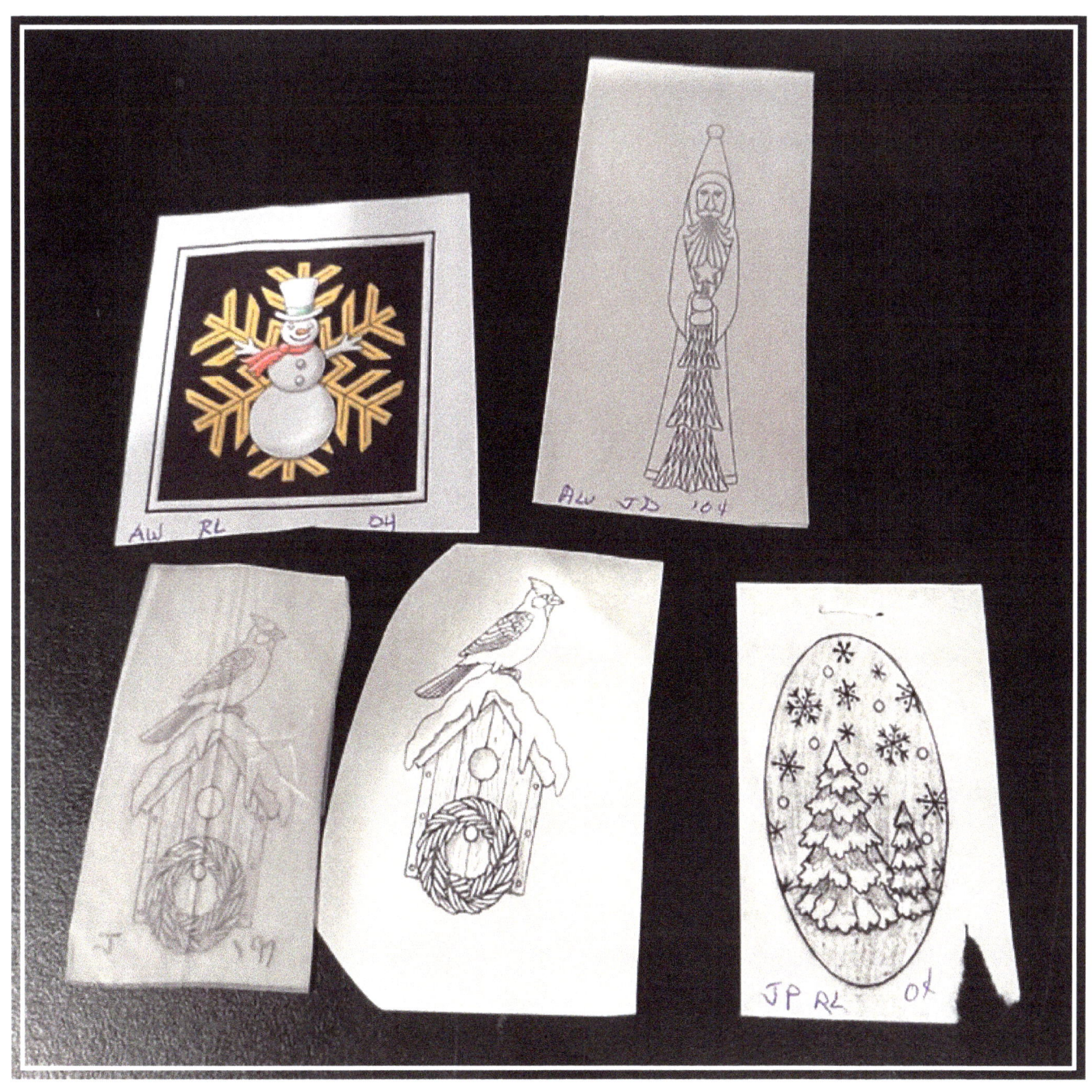

Different designs: snowman, Alan Weimer, designer, Raphael Lopes, model maker, 2004;
Santa, Alan Weimer, designer, Jim Dumachelle, model maker, 2004;
Christmas Trees in Snow, Janet Parker Prata, designer, Raphael Lopes, model maker, 2004

Lighthouse, Alan Weimer, designer, possibly Tony Martins, model maker, 2003
Frog in Chair, Alan Weimer, designer, Raphael Lopes, model maker, 1999
Fish, Janet Parker Prata, designer, Raphael Lopes, model maker, 2005

Marion Firmani, designer, Peter? Model maker. 1999

Alan Weimer, designer, David Lisker, model maker, 2002

Alan Weimer, designer, Raphael Lopes, model maker 1995

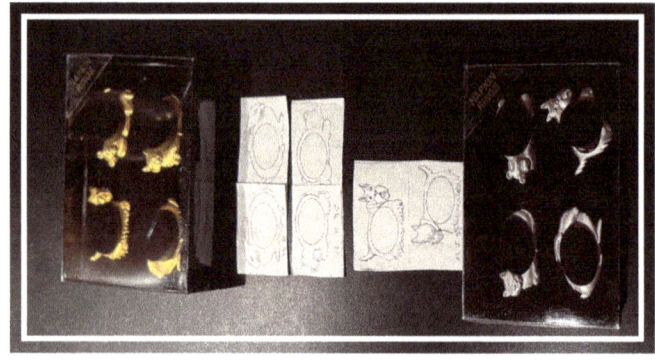

Alan Weimer, designer, Raphael Lopes, designer 2002

Alan Weimer, designer, Jim Dumachelle, model maker, 1996 Note how the same car was used to carry a Christmas tree in the finished pin, and a canoe in the illustration

Flying Witch, Nunzio Izzo, designer, 1993

Alan Weimer, designer, Jim Dumachelle, model maker, 1998

Alan Weimer, designer, Jim Dumachelle, model maker

Marian Firmani, designer, 1998

Leaf bracelet, Janet Parker Prata, designer 2003

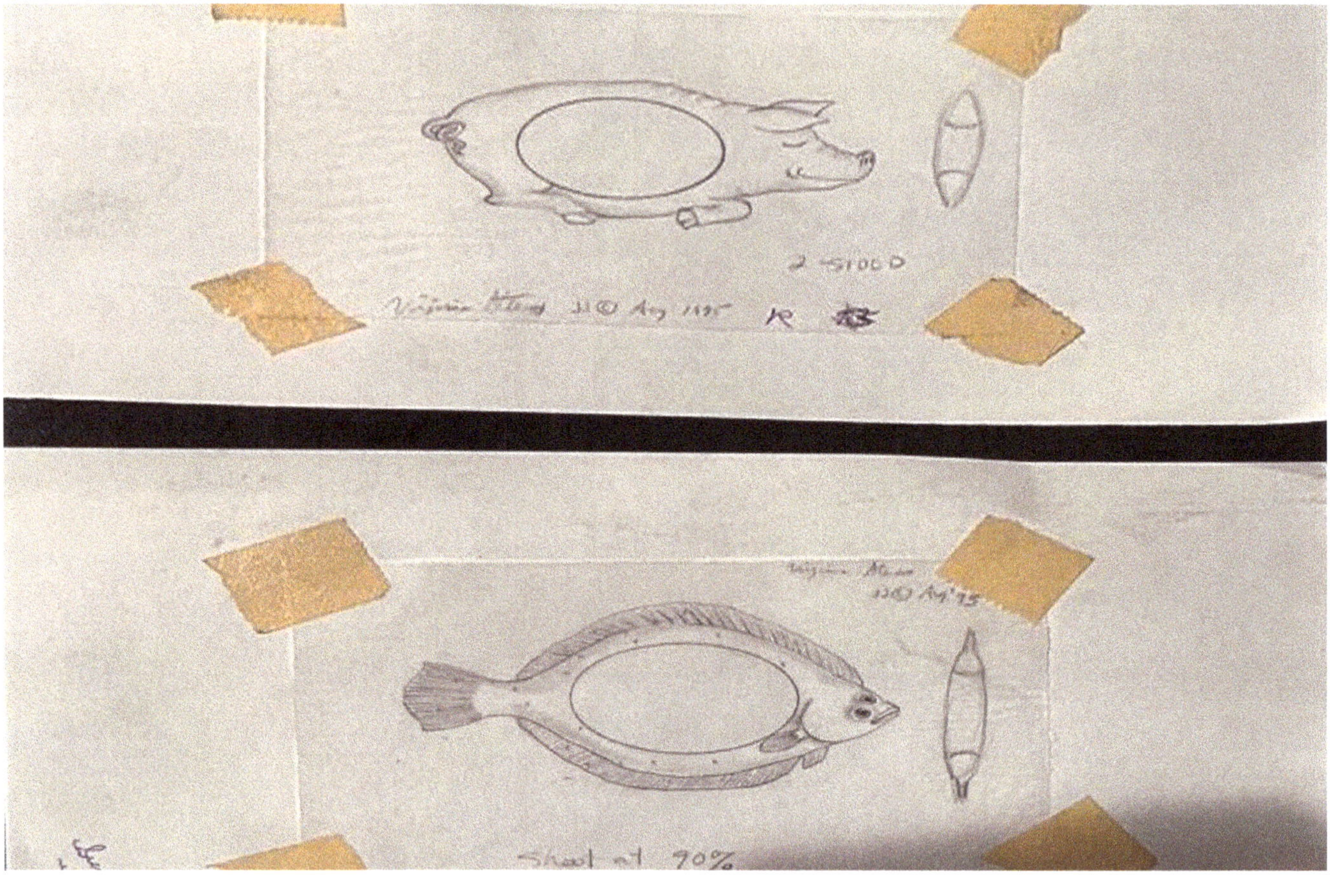

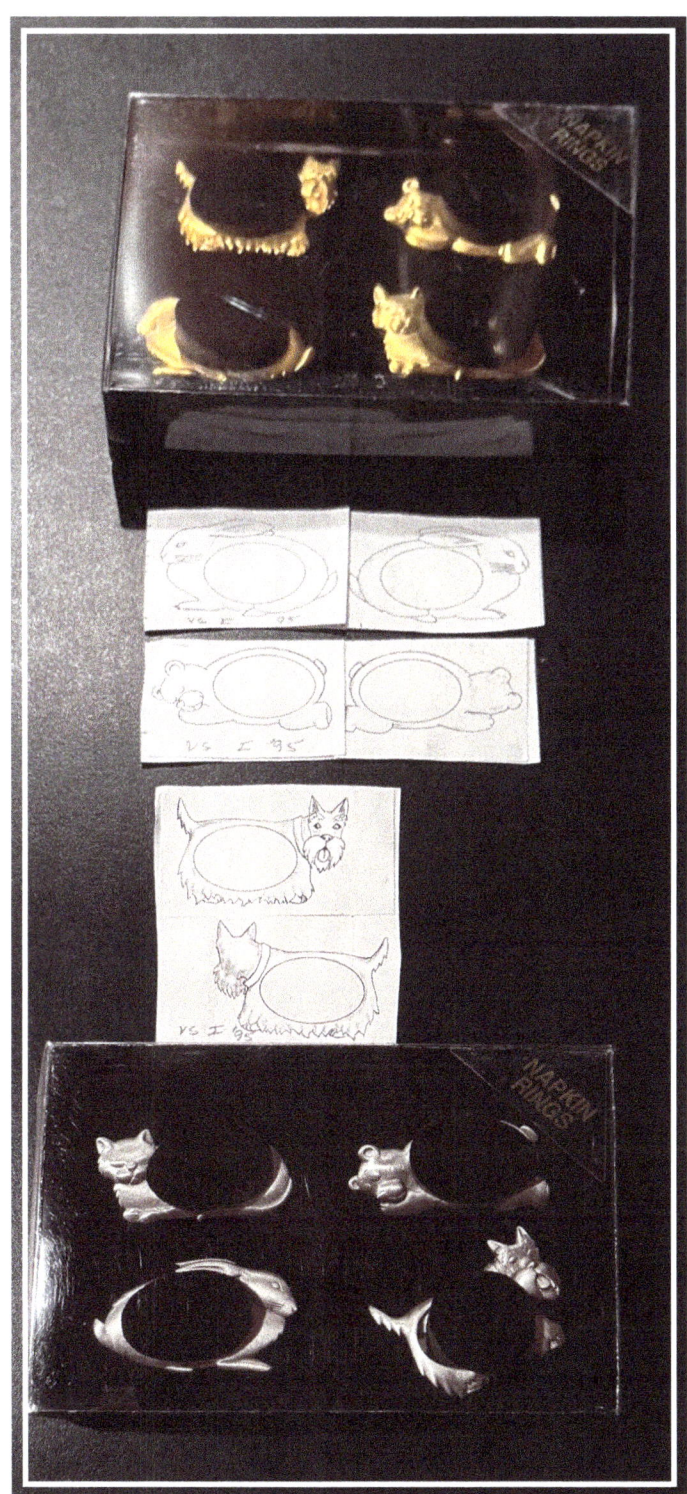

Napkin Rings Even though JJ is best known for its wonderful brooch designs, they made other items, such as these clever napkin rings. Both sets are from 1995, and were designed by Virginia Stevens and made by model maker Isaac Newar

Boo and ghost sketches, designer, Janet Parker Prata

PAGE 129

Ms. Dee This is a wonderful example of Alan Weimer's design of the clever Ms. Dee boxes containing coordinating necklaces and earrings 1992 Jim Dumachelle, model maker

Work order for beaded stick pin – Here is an example of a JJ pin using beads.
Ann Donahue, designer, David Lisker, model maker, 1999

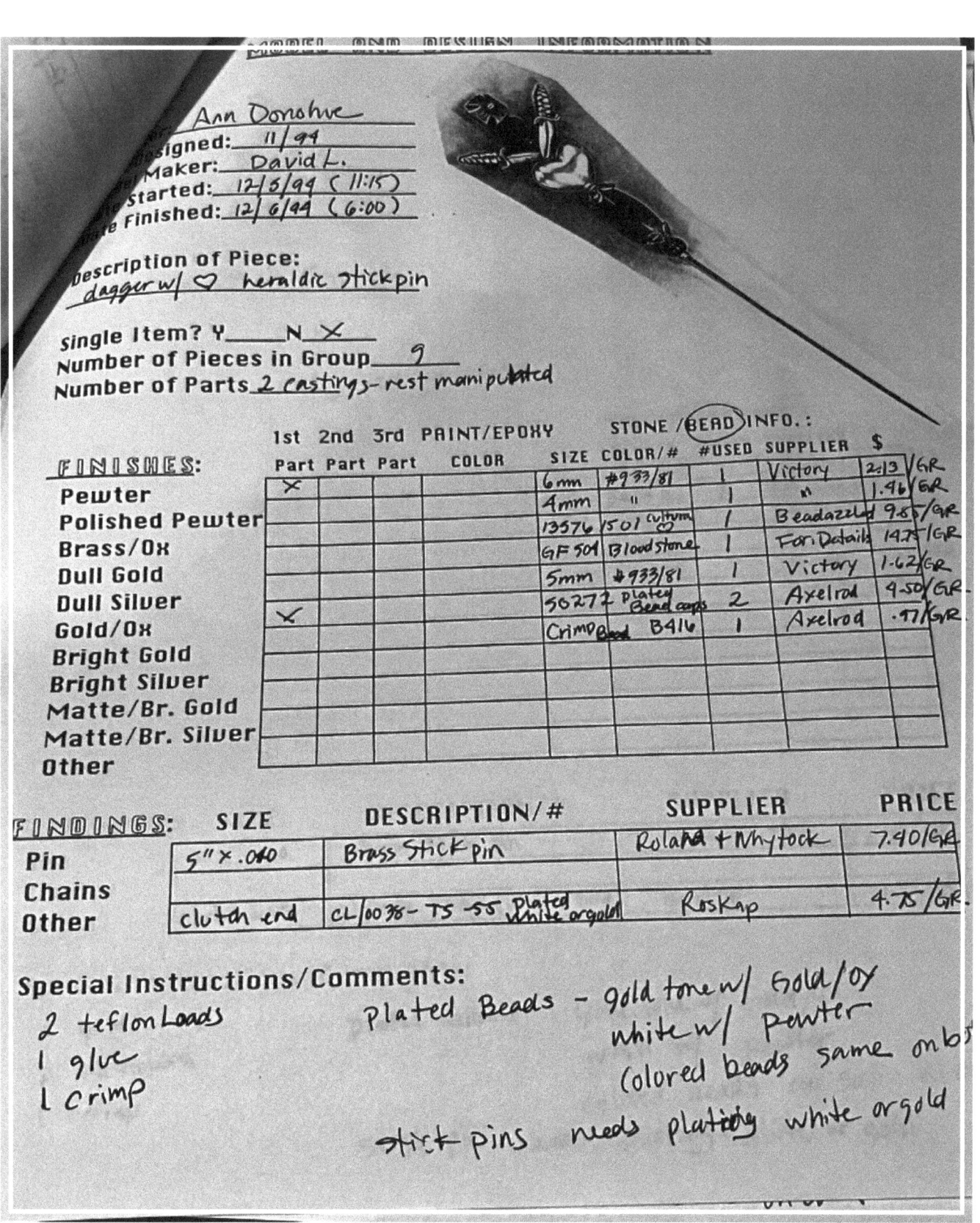

*Another work order for a beaded stick pin – Ann Donahue,
Designer, David Lisker, model maker 1999*

Heron Art Nouveau design quartz clock 1993

These clocks were also designed by Alan Weimer

Another non jewelry item - quartz clock in an Art Nouveau design 1992

MODEL AND DESIGN INFORMATION

Designer: GINNY
Date Designed: _____
Model Maker: ISAAC
Date Started: _____
Date Finished: May 19/97   1600 HRS

DESCRIPTION OF PIECE:
Cat Book Mark

Single Item? Y ____ N ✗
Number of Pieces in Group __6__
Number of Parts _____

FINISHES:

	1st Part	2nd Part	3rd Part
Pewter	✗		
Polished Pewter			
Brass/Ox	✗		
Dull Gold	✗		
Dull Silver			
Gold/Ox			
Bright Gold			
Bright Silver			
Matte/Br. Gold			
Matte/Br. Silver			
Other			

Paint/Epoxy: Color

Stone/Bead Info:

Size	Color/#	#Used	Supplier	Price

FINDINGS:

	Size	Description/#	#Used	Supplier	Price
Pin					
Chains					
Other		1198 - hole Stainless	1	Norwood Findings Co. Inc.	$9.00/g

Special Instructions/Comments: finding is swedged on unplated for pewter finish

MODEL AND DESIGN INFORMATION

Designer: Ginny & Alan
Date Designed: _____
Model Maker: Keith
Date Started: 5/8/97
Date Finished: 5/15/97

DESCRIPTION OF PIECE:

#1 Bookmark

Single Item? Y___ N_X_
Number of Pieces in Group _6_
Number of Parts _____

FINISHES:	1st Part	2nd Part	3rd Part	Paint/Epoxy: Color			Stone/Bead Info: Size	Color/#	#Used	Supplier
Pewter	X									
Polished Pewter										
Brass/Ox	X									
Dull Gold	X									
Dull Silver										
Gold/Ox										
Bright Gold										
Bright Silver										
Matte/Br. Gold										
Matte/Br. Silver										
Other										

FINDINGS:

	Size	Description/#	#Used	Supplier
Pin				
Chains		1198 - Hole stainless	1	Norwood Finding
Other				

Special Instructions/Comments: finding is swedged on
☆ Leave unplated for pewter finish

Examples of work orders

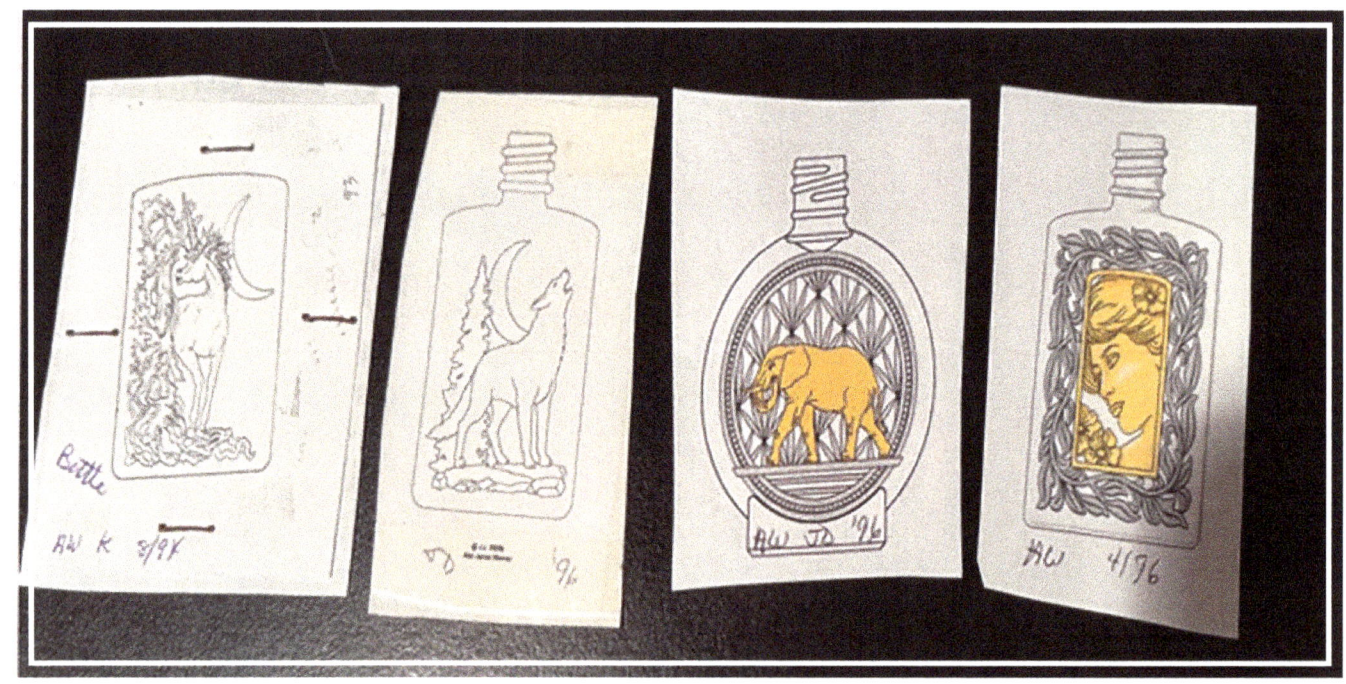

More perfume bottle designs

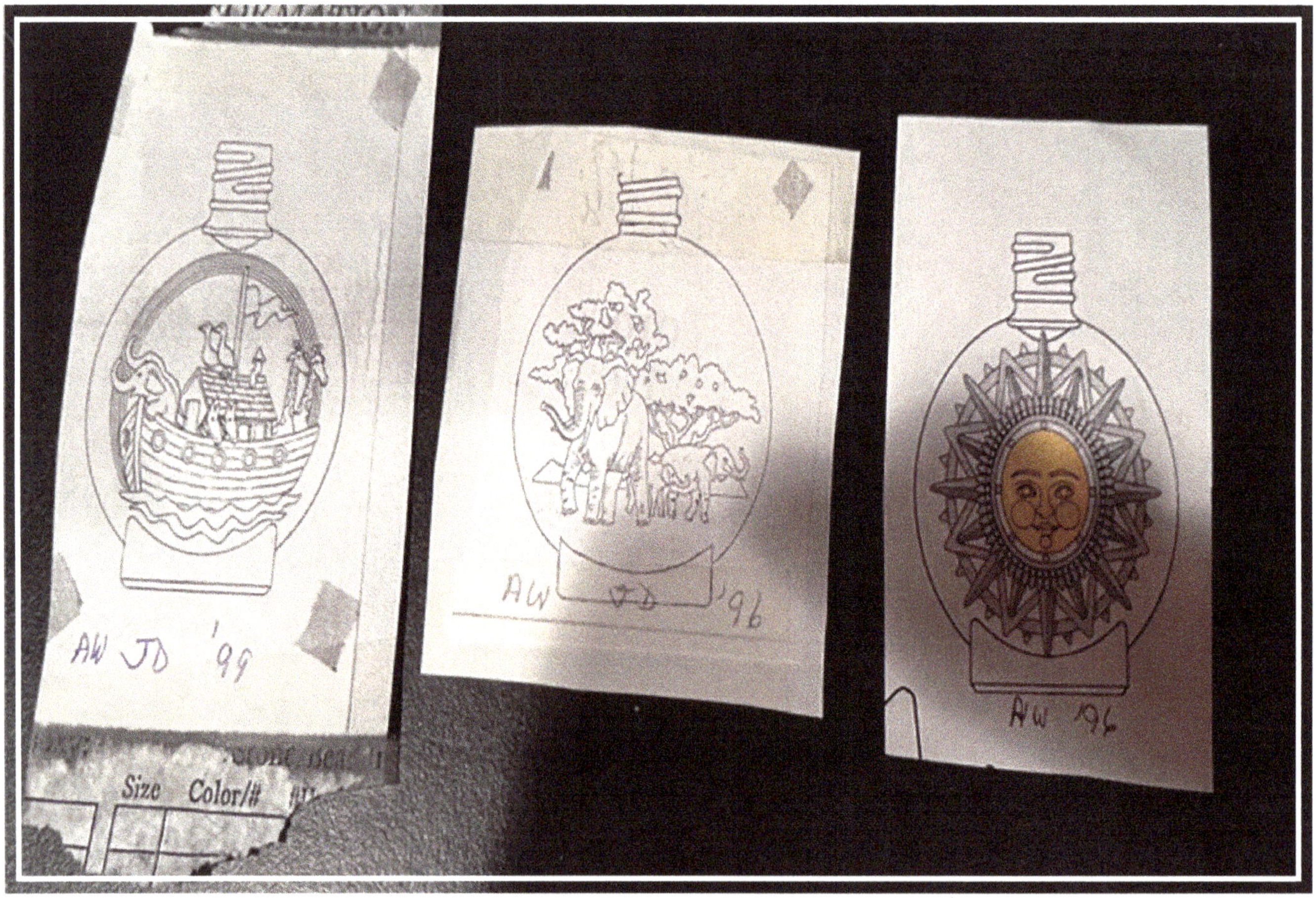

Perfume bottle designs Alan Weimer, designer; Jim Dumachelle, model maker, 1996, 1999

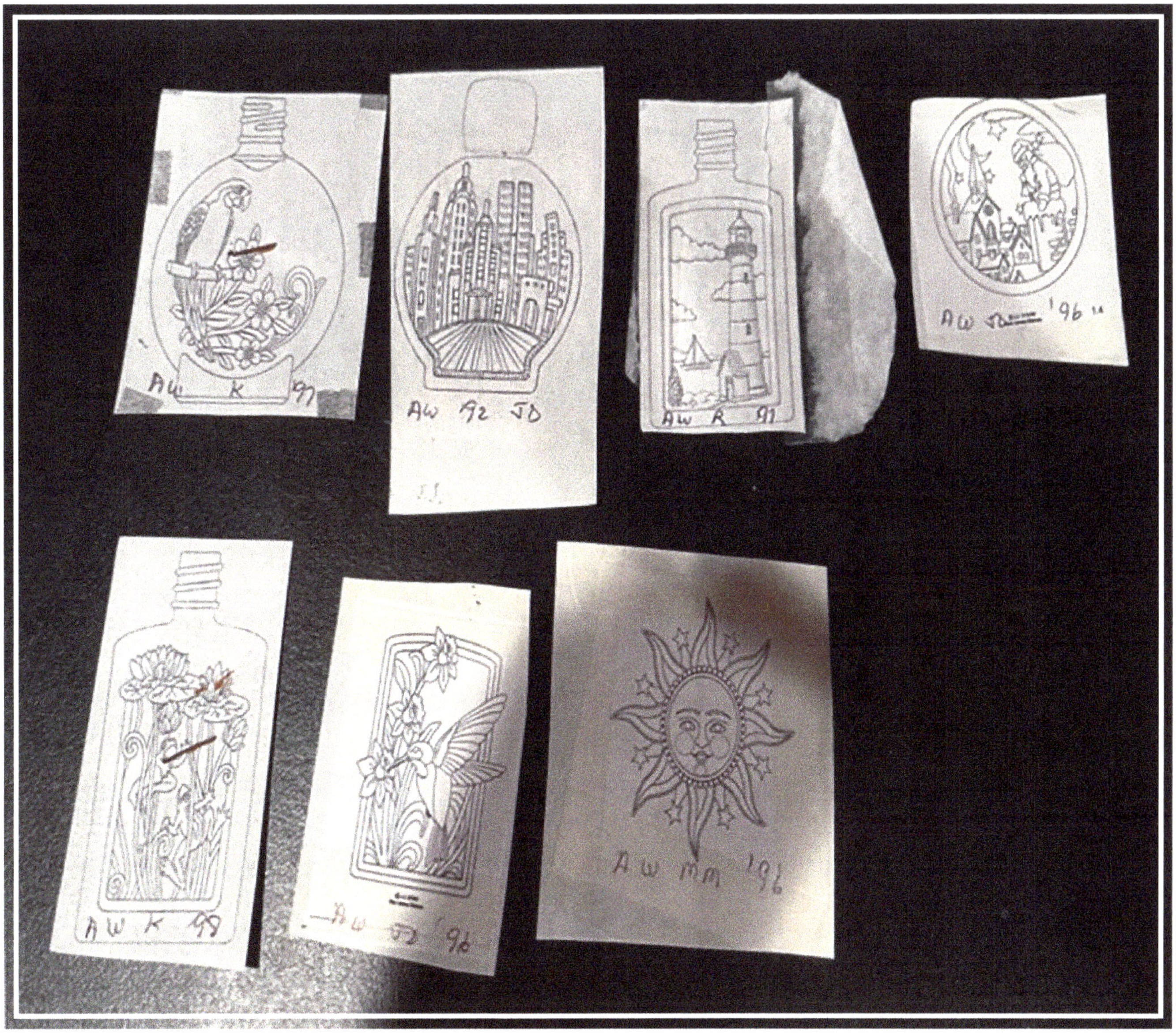

Perfume bottle designs, all by Alan Weimer; Model makers, left to right, Top row: Keith Curvelo, 1997; Jim Dumachelle, 1992; Raphael Lopes, 1997; Jim Dumachelle, 1996. Bottom row: Keith Curvelo, 1995; Jim Dumachelle, 1996; Mike Manni, 1996

Apparently, JJ got its glass perfume bottles from the ABA Packaging Corp.

Perfume bottle, left, Alan Weimer, designer, Jim Dumachelle, model maker, 1996;
Right, Ginny Stevens and Alan Weimer, designers, Jim Dumachelle, model Maker, 1994   *Alan Weimer, designer*

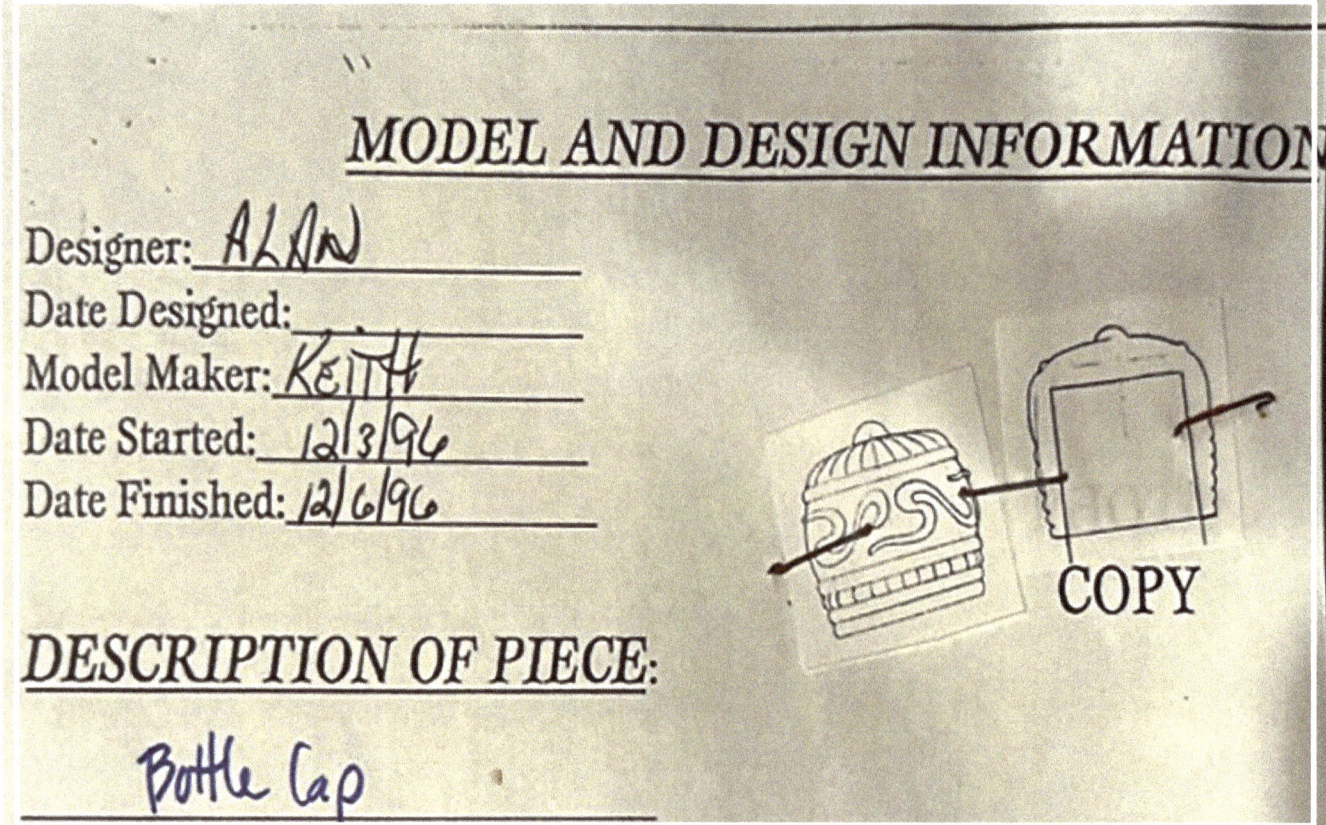

Perfume bottle cap design, 1996, Alan Weimer, designer, Keith Curvelo, model maker

More perfume bottle designs, all designed by Alan Weimer. Various model makers and years, as noted on the pictures

Mouse in a cabinet!
Alan Weimer, designer; Jim Dumachelle, model maker, 1993

Money in a safe! Alan Weimer, designer, Jim Dumachelle, model maker

Perfume bottle cap design, 1996, Alan Weimer, designer, Richard D., model maker

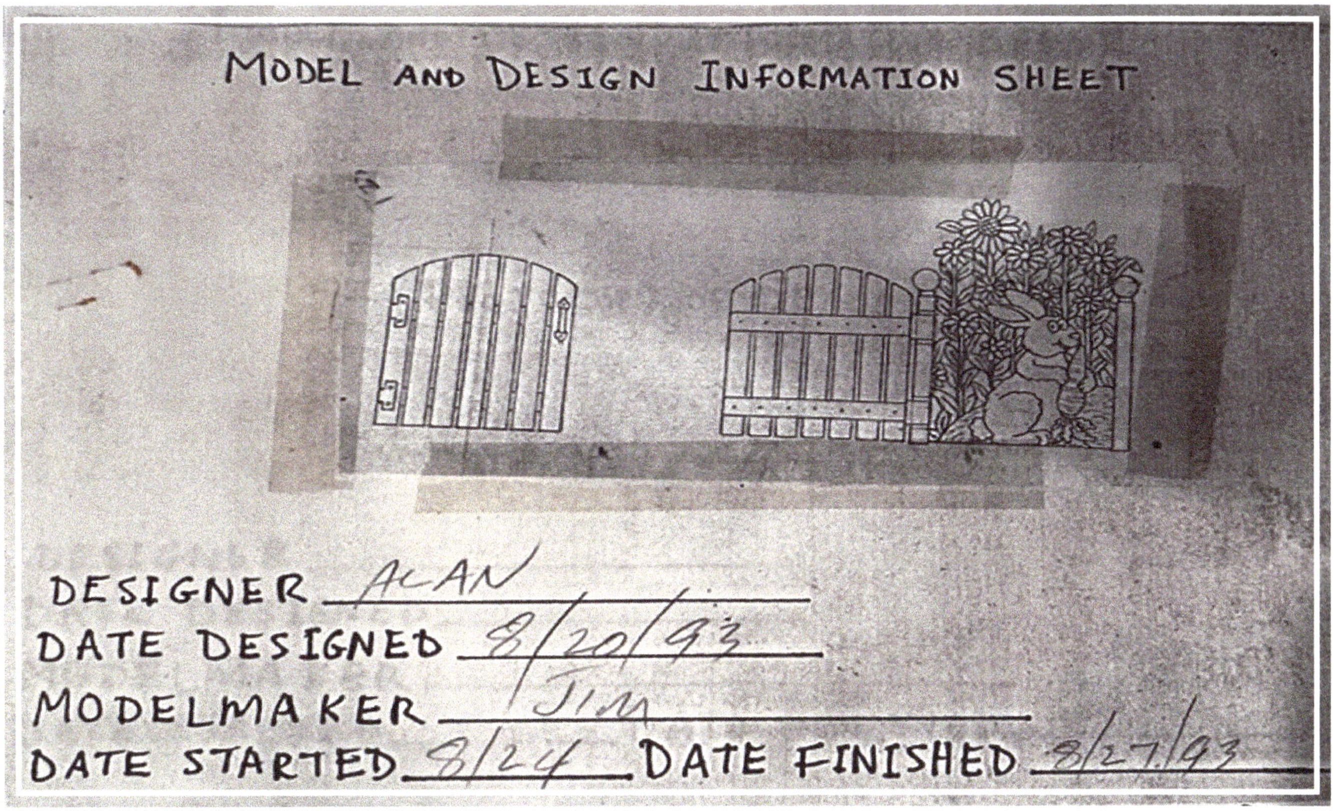

MODEL AND DESIGN INFORMATION SHEET

DESIGNER ALAN
DATE DESIGNED 8/20/93
MODELMAKER JIM
DATE STARTED 8/24 DATE FINISHED 8/27/93

Bunny behind a closing gate, one of JJ's opening door pins. Alan Weimer, designer; Jim Dumachelle, model maker, 1993

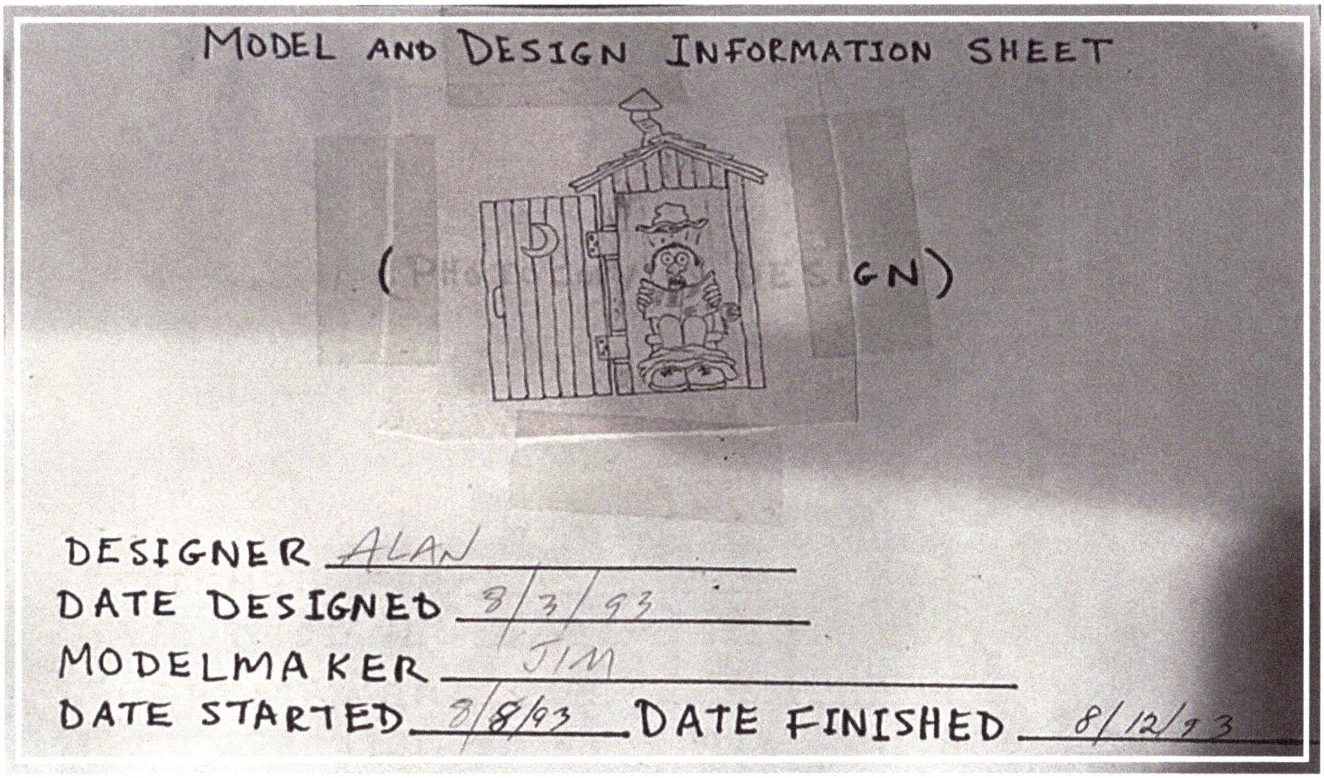

MODEL AND DESIGN INFORMATION SHEET

DESIGNER ALAN
DATE DESIGNED 8/3/93
MODELMAKER JIM
DATE STARTED 8/8/93 DATE FINISHED 8/12/93

Oops, opened the outhouse door too soon! Alan Weimer, designer; Jim Dumachelle, model maker, 1993

Dragon and fish magnifying glass, both Ginny Stevens, designer, Jim Dumachelle, model maker, 1997

Ornament Janet Parker Prata, designer, Ralph Lopez, model maker

Spoon or scoop creations

Sandal bracelet design, work in progress-there is a question for designer Alan, "Will this hang right?", and another question about color

Check out the swimsuits! Janet Parker Prata, designer

Women's Accessories bracelet Janet Parker Prata, designer; Rapahel Lopes, model maker, 2004

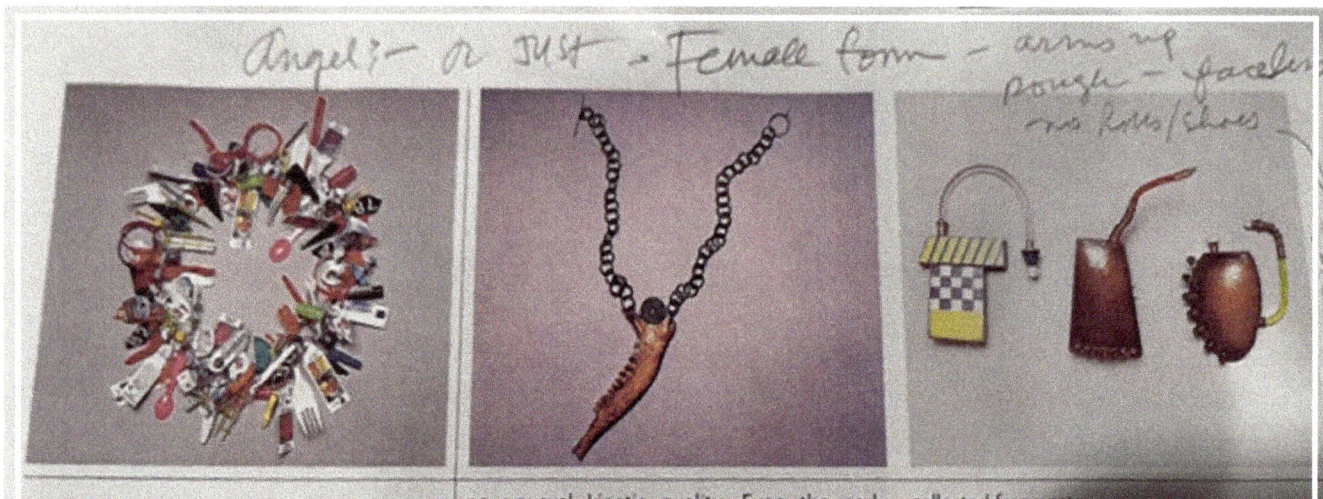

"THE JEWELRY OF ROBERT EBENDORF: A RETROSPECTIVE OF FORTY YEARS"
GALLERY OF ART AND DESIGN, NCSU,
RALEIGH, NORTH CAROLINA
JANUARY 16-MARCH 9, 2003

ARKANSAS ART CENTER, LITTLE ROCK
MAY 18-JUNE 22, 2003

RENWICK GALLERY OF THE SMITHSONIAN AMERICAN ART MUSEUM,
WASHINGTON, D.C.

an unusual kinetic quality. Even the early objects—tightly circumscribed symmetrical shapes—dance with an interior energy. The raised silver forms of berry spoon, gavel, umbrella handle, and such are rendered talismanic by the activity of their pierced or applied ornamentation. In this early work we also begin to sense Ebendorf's extreme sensitivity to the emotive and expressive powers of materials, especially as they interact with one another. Sterling silver with ebony says something quite different from silver with walnut.

By the early 1970s, Ebendorf's palette of collected fragments.

Fortunately, the ideas and the zest soon returned, better and bolder. There are chunky necklaces of globe-like handmade beads look like Ebendorf just grabbed up the planet loop around a woman's neck. There are necklaces as gaudy and large as leis, made from brightly colored SoCal beach trash; and one equally large but demurely composed of slender silver trimmed with delicate gold wire spirals and pearls. Another series of necklaces with shaped pendants shows Ebendorf in scavenger mode. Precious metals, coat

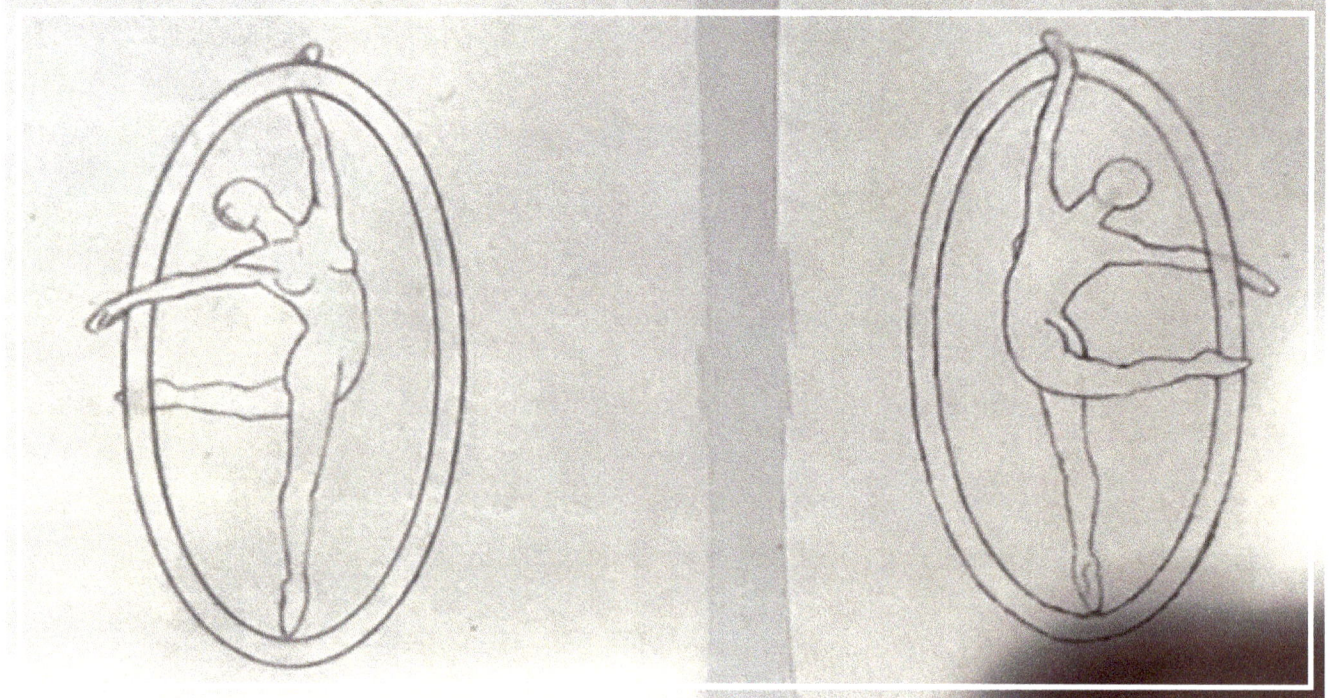

Sketches by Janet Parker Prata

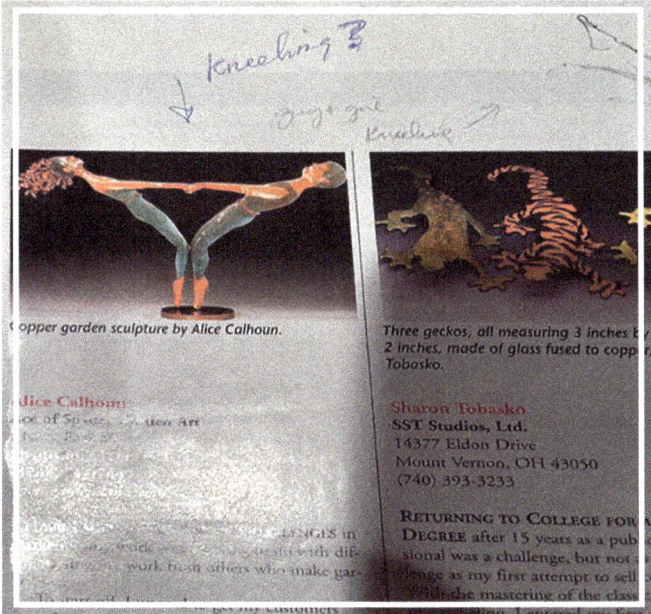

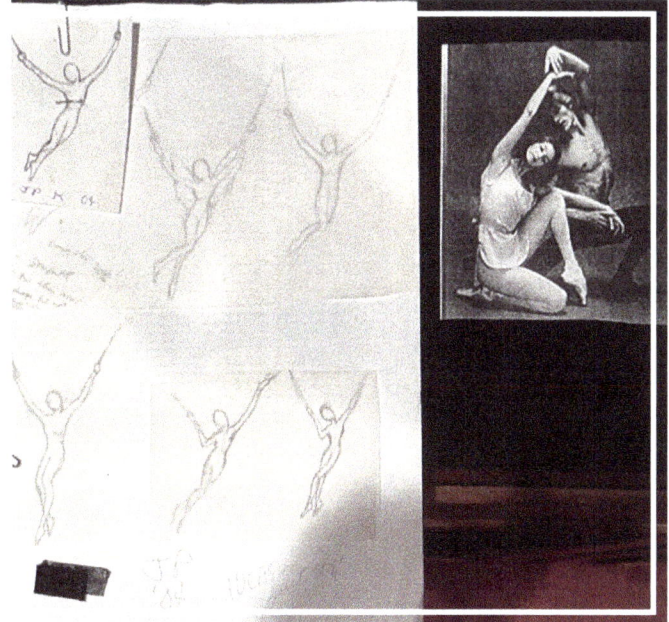

Dance inspiration Janet Parker Prata designer 2004

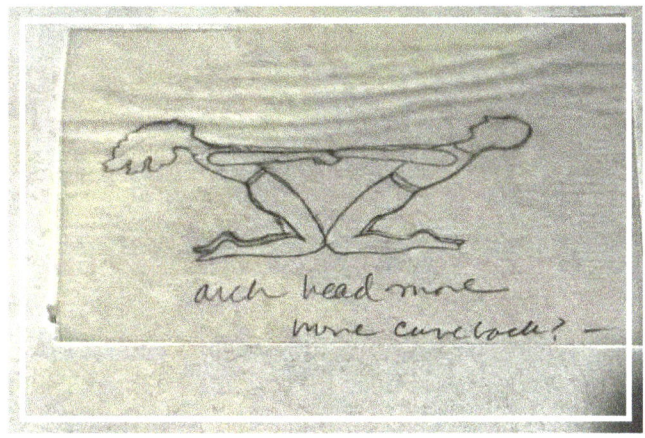

Jewelry designs inspired by current trends. As Alan Weimer stated, JJ designers would look at magazines for inspiration, as they showed what trends were of interest to consumers.

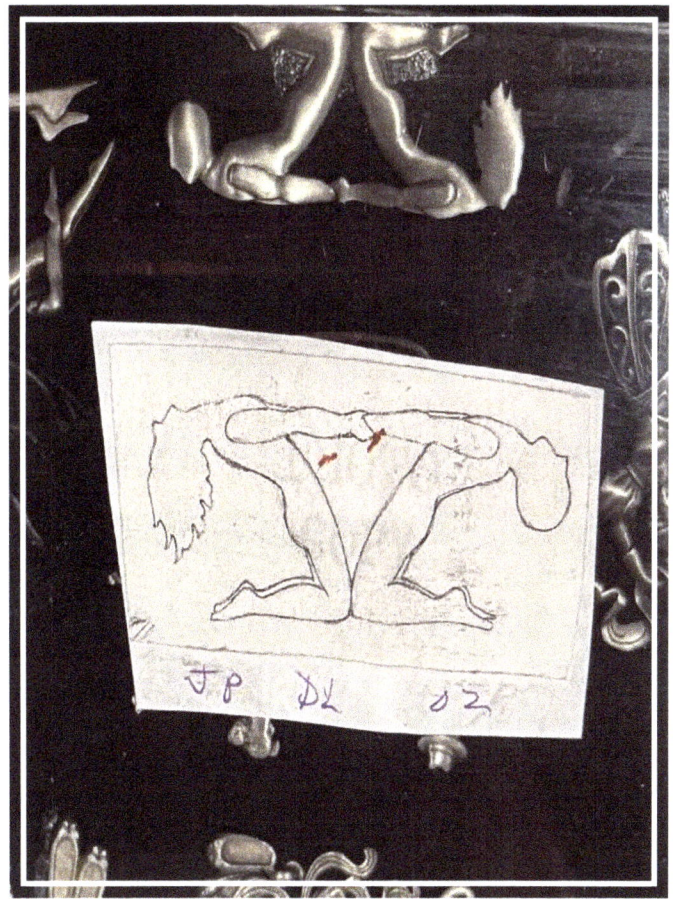

The finished product; Janet Parker Prata, designer; David Lisker, model maker. 2002

Skiing Anyone? Ginny Stevens, designer;
Keith Curvelo, model maker, 1994

Alan Weimer, designer; David Lisker, model maker, 2003

Sewing pin with dangles Ginny Stevens, designer;
David Lisker, model maker 1994

Palm trees Janet Parker Prata, designer;
Not clear on model maker, 2005

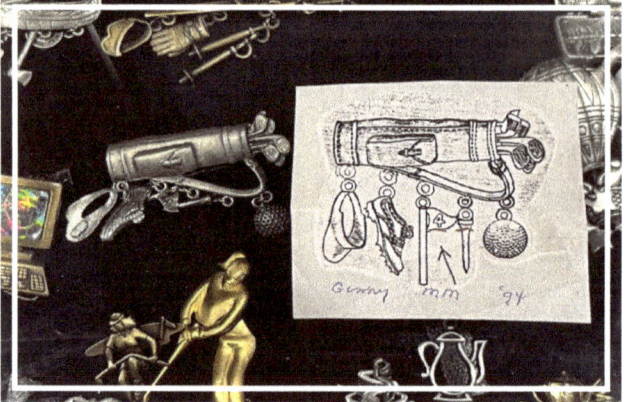

Golfing Ginny Stevens, designer;
Mike Manni, model maker, 1994

Alan Weimer, designer; Isaac Newar, model maker, 1998

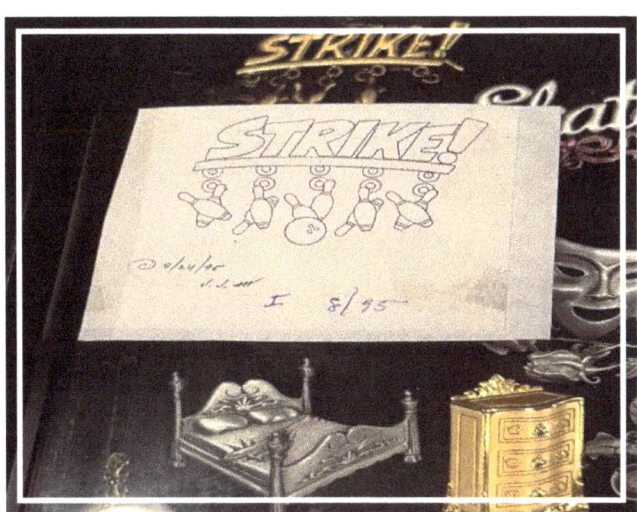

This bowling pin is from 1995

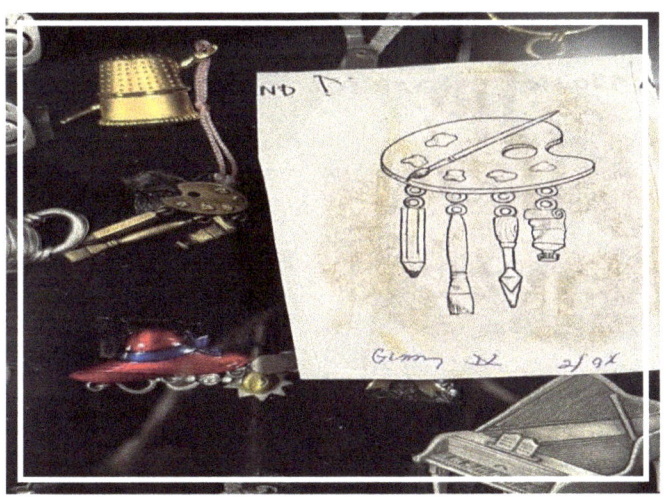

Ginny Stevens, designer; David Lisker, model maker, 1994

Gambling Pin Don Salliby, model maker, 1995

*Dutch treat! Alan Weimer, designer;
Raphael Lopes, model maker, 2003*

*JJ Humor - internet surfing! Alan Weimer, designer;
Isaac Newar, model maker, 1996*

Dance! Alan Weimer, designer; David Lisker, model maker, 1997

Antique Car, Alan Weimer, designer; Raphael Lopes, model maker, 1999

Masquerade! 1994 Not sure regarding designer and model maker

Swing!, Alan Weimer, designer; Raphael Lopes, model maker, 1996

An example of JJ organization – these are tack pin backs for their Christmas moose pin

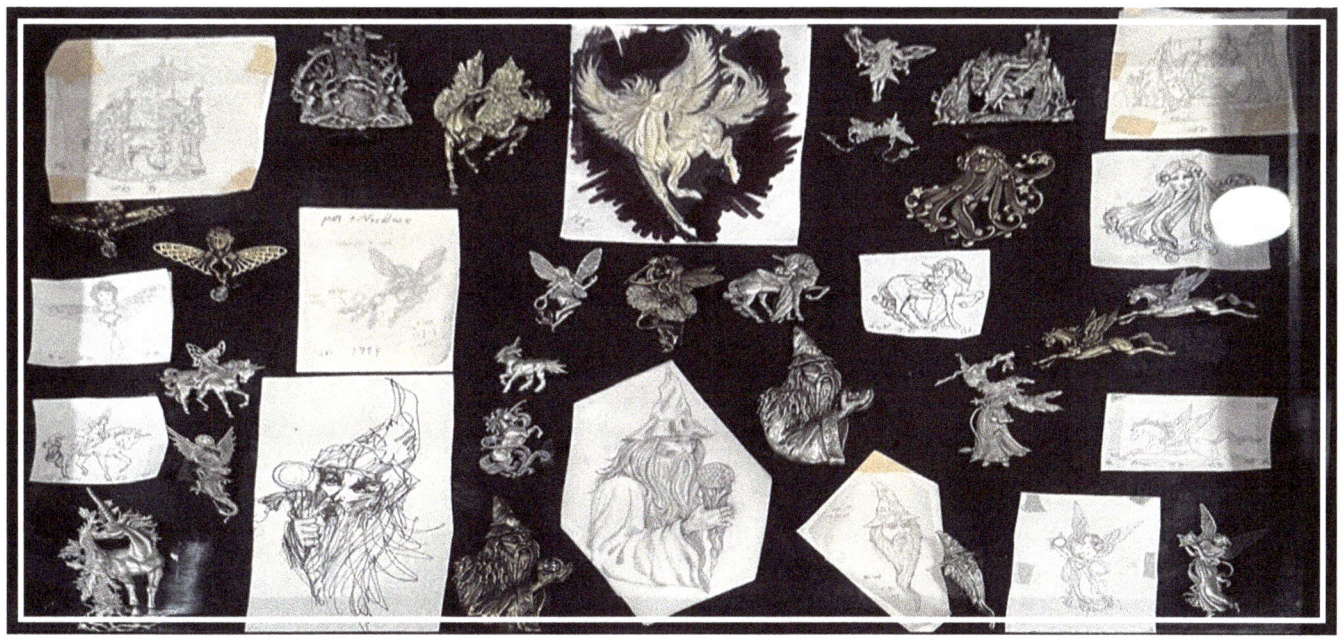

Designer Nunzio Izzo made many of the fantastic mythological designs that JJ is known for – wizards, Pegasus, unicorns, etc, but other designers were involved as well.

Nunzio Izzo designed the winged horse; 1991; Alan Weimer designed the long bearded wizard in the bottom right

PAGE 149

Now this is a creepy witch! Sketch by Nunzio Izzo.

Different designs – Top Row, Alan Weimer, designer; Keith Curvelo, model maker, 2005; Bottom row, left, Alan Weimer, designer, Peter C., model maker, 1999, bottom row right, Marion Firmani, designer, Isaac Newar, model maker

Thimble design; Ginny Stevens, designer; David Lisker, model maker, 1995

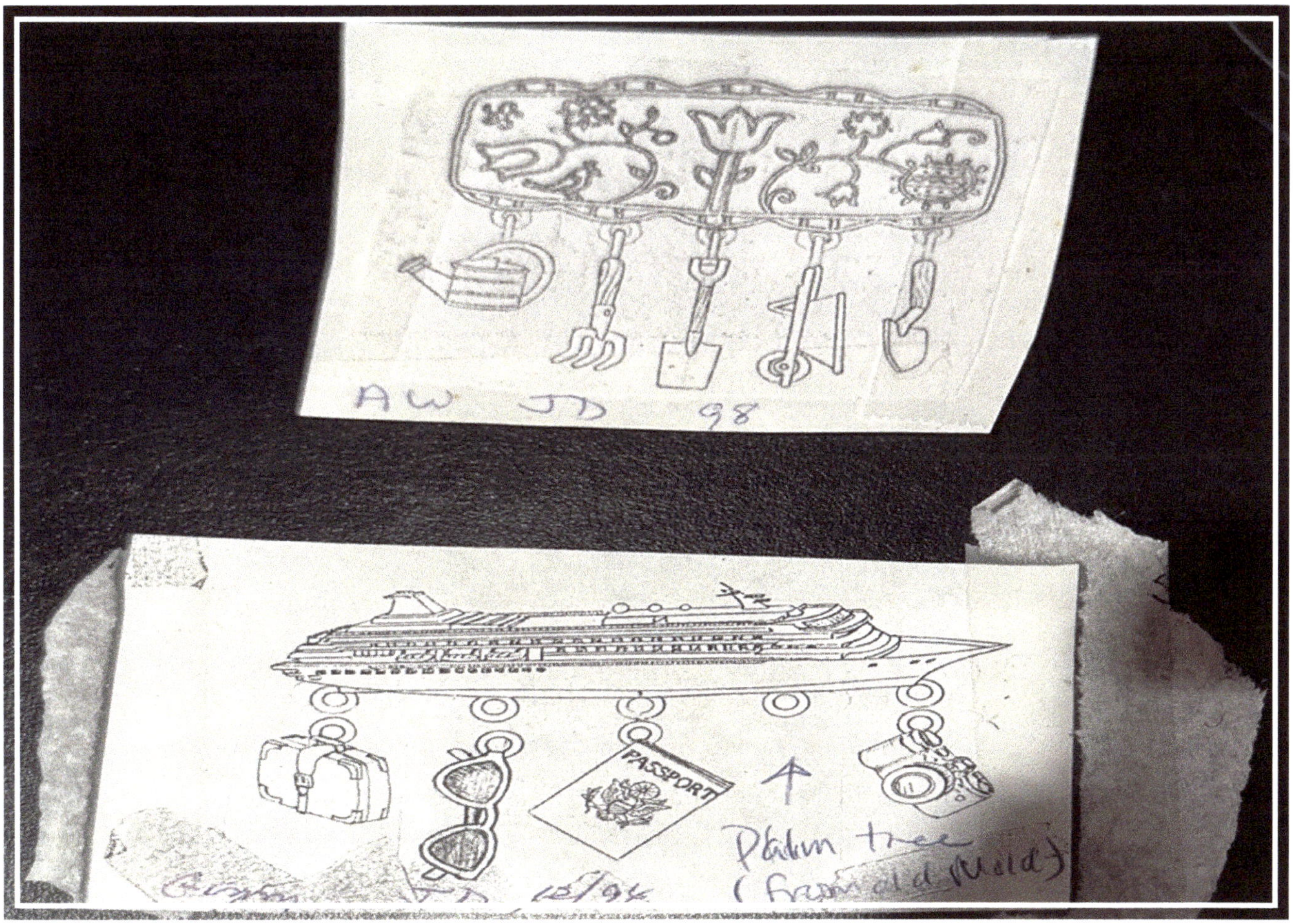

Top: Alan Weimer, designer; Jim Dumachelle, model maker, 1998; Bottom, Ginny Stevens, designer, Jim Dumachelle, model maker, 1996. Note how they were using an old palm tree mold for the dangle on the ship pin.

PAGE 151

Greyhound, Janet Parker Prata, designer, Jim Dumachelle, model maker, 2005; Picture frame dangle from bone, Alan Weimer, designer, 1993; Scampering Dog, Nunzio Izzo Designer, 1995; Poodle, Ginny Stevens, 1993; Dog House Picture, Alan Weimer, designer, Isaac Newar, model maker; 1999; My Best Friend heart picture frame, Ginny Stevens, designer, 1994; Dog House Picture, Alan Weimer, designer, Isaac Newar, model maker, 1999; German Shepard, Janet Parker Prata, designer, 1990; Woof woof picture frame, Ginny Stevens, designer, Mike Manni, model maker,1999; Running dog, red spots, Alan Weimer, designer, Keith Curvelo, model maker; 1993; Dog with stocking, fireplace, Janet Parker Prata, model maker T?, 2002; dachshund with bow, Janet Parker Prata, designer, 2001; Dog Lover, Marion Firmani, designer, Jim Dumachelle, model maker, 1998; Running Dog, Janet Parker Prata, designer, 1990; St. Francis with animals and "Happily Ever After (2 dogs in love)", designer, Janet Parker Prata.

Going to the Dogs! Back of Dog-Tony Martins, model maker, 1991; Standing Dog, Janet Parker Prata, designer, 1990s; Santa petting dog, Janet Parker Prata designer, Jim Dumachelle, model maker, 2002-2003; Running dog, Janet Parker Prata, designer, 2005; Dog with Flag, Alan Weimer, designer, Keith Curvelo, model maker, 2002; Cocker Spaniel, Janet Parker Prata, model maker, 2000; Picture Pin Award Ribbon, Alan Weimer, designer, Isaac Newar, model maker, 1993

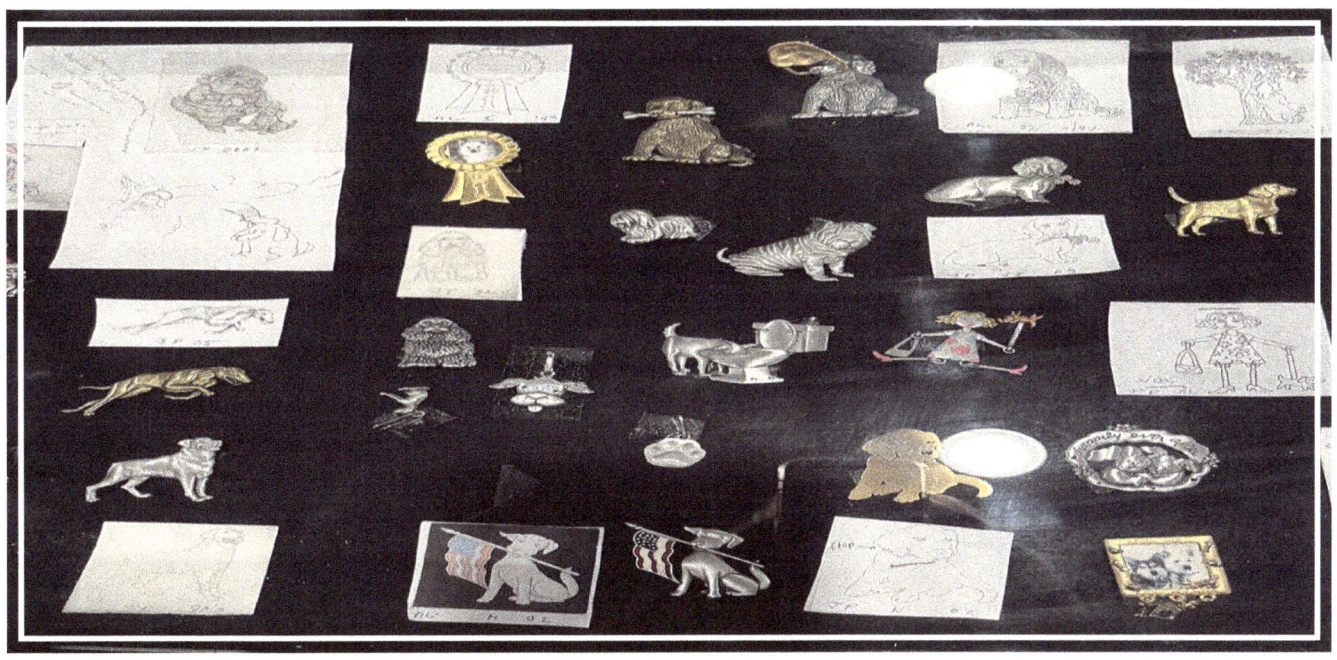

Woman in flowered dress, Janet Parker Prata, designer, Raphael Lopes, model maker, 2005; sitting dog, Janet Parker Prata, designer, Keith Curvelo, model maker, 2002

Wonderful advertisement of JJ's Artifacts line-look at the definition on the mountain lion! All the designs in this poster, as well as the stylized "J" and the Artifacts logo, were by Alan Weimer.

Santa petting dog, Ginny Stevens, designer, 1995; Woman with house And dog; Janet Parker Prata, designer, Dan Salliby, model maker, 2001

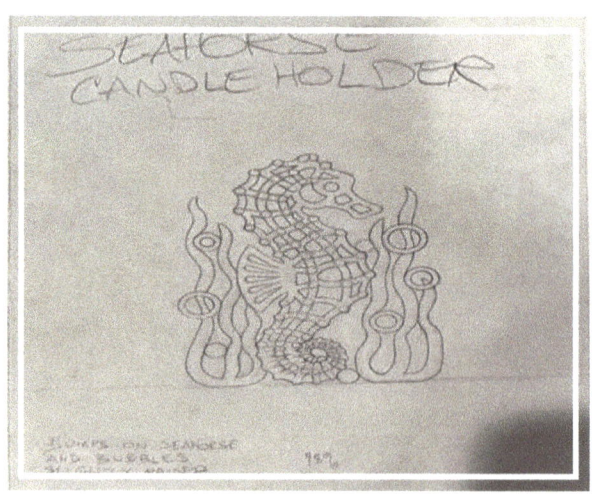

A seahorse candle holder, designer Alan Weimer

Fruit pins, late 1990s-author Nancy Rosendal, hiding in the corner

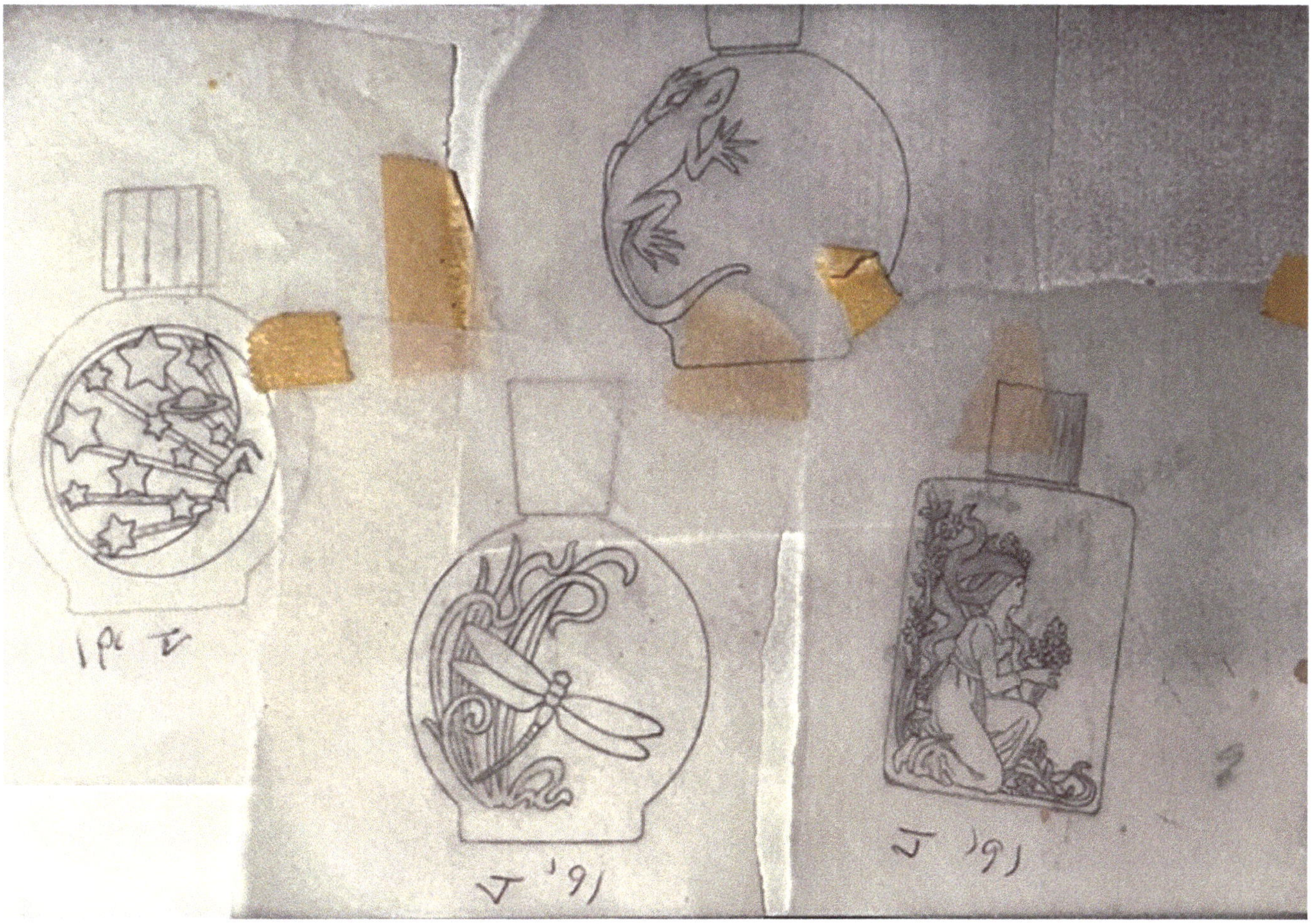

CHRISTMAS AND RELIGION

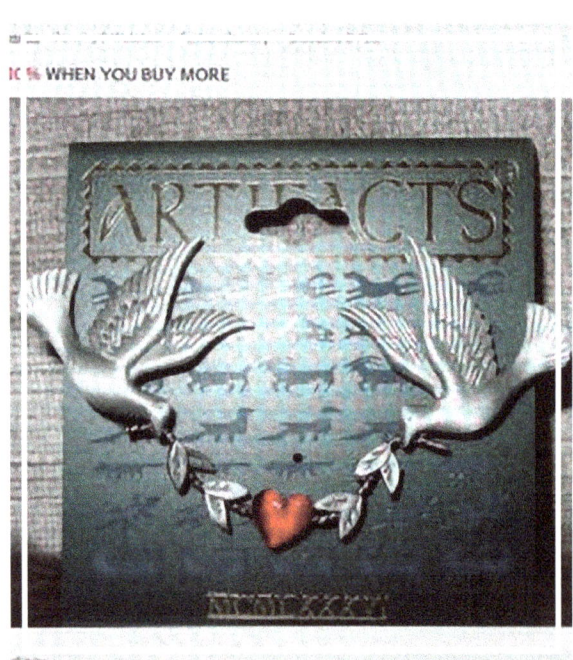

Janet Parker Prata, designer

One of the trends that JJ picked up on was the Red Hat Society. This is an organization that encourages women in their quest to get the most out of life. Their website states "We support women in the pursuit of Fun, Friendship, Freedom, Fitness and the Fulfillment of lifelong dreams." The organization began in 1998, so the Red Hat Lady pins likely date to 1999 or 2000. The other gold tone pin, of the elegant woman with a fan, was and is, a popular design.

Red Hat Society inspiration 1

The Fall wreath pin, adorned with apples and sunflowers, appears to be of a similar era as the fruit pins depicted on page 155

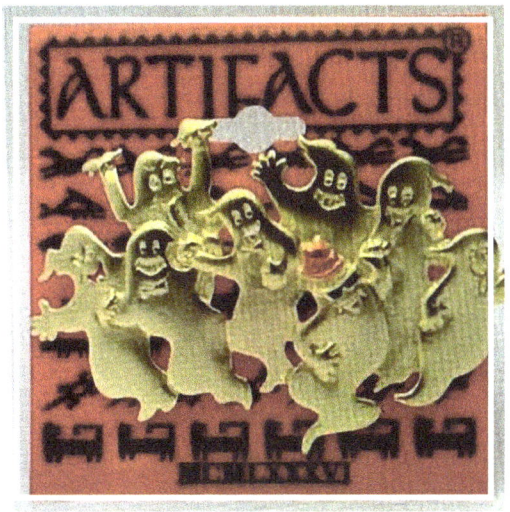

Janet Parker Prata, designer

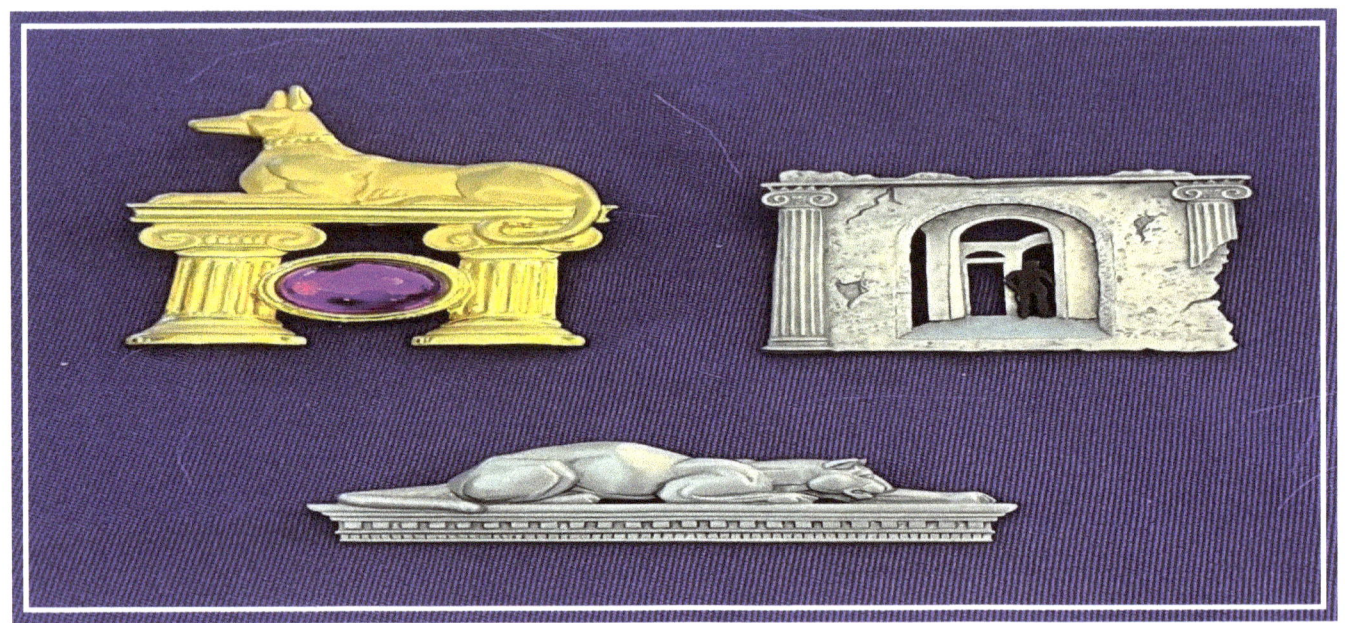

Walk like an Egyptian...

Skylines – flying pigs, flying saucers and dragons! The NYC skyline dates to 1988 according to copyright lists.

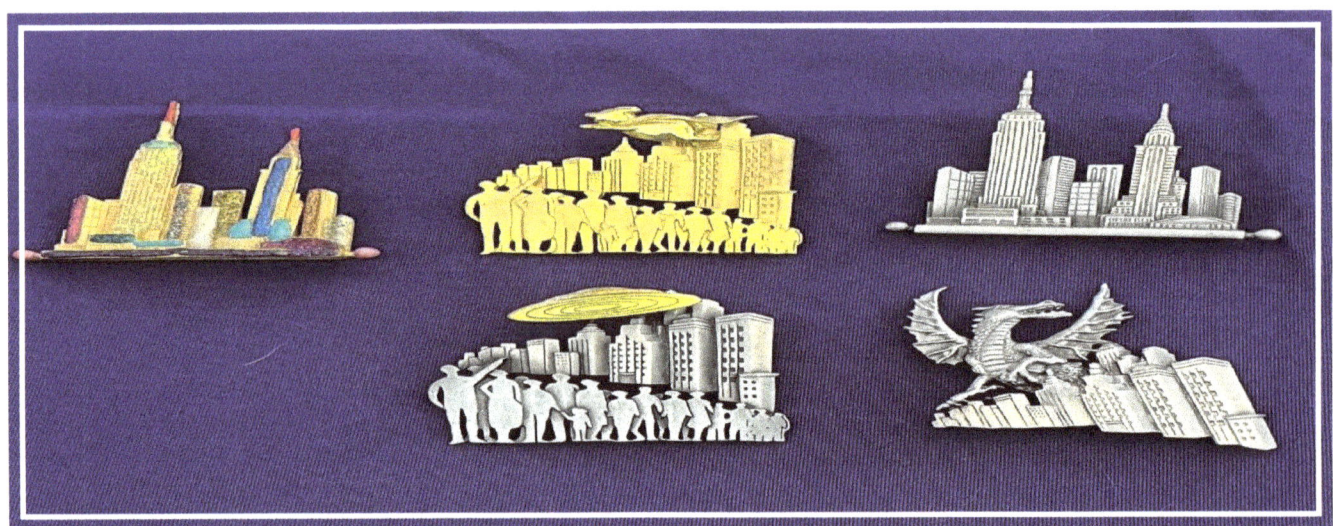

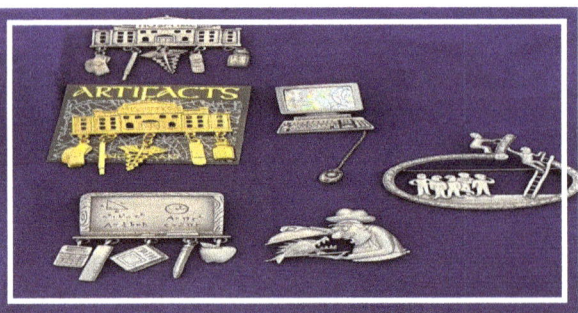

Mystical and mythological

Illustrations of the same brooch with different finishes

Alan Weimer, designer

Fairies designed by Alan Weimer, Pegasus designed by Nunzio Izzo

Ornate designs. The first design shows a cherub in a fanciful setting, set with green cabochons. The second depicts a woman gazing at a shooting star, set with iridescent cabochons. This pin seems to be inspired by Gordon's design.

Wonderful designs-a woman's profile against a crescent moon and sunrays; a matte gold finish gingko leaf, set with an iridescent cabochon; Dancing folks in the moonlight, two tone

Dancers under moon pin, designer, Janet Parker Prata

PAGE 169

One of the areas in which JJ excelled was the female form. Here you see the lovely profile of artist Alan Weimer's wife, along with film noir images of women. You have to love the pearls used as bubbles in the bathtub pins, and the humor of Lady Godiva on her horse! The door pin opens to show the woman walking her whippet.

The bubble bath woman is from 1991, and the designer was Nunzio Izzo

Professions-hospitals, medical, computer, construction, teaching and a true Chef's surprise!

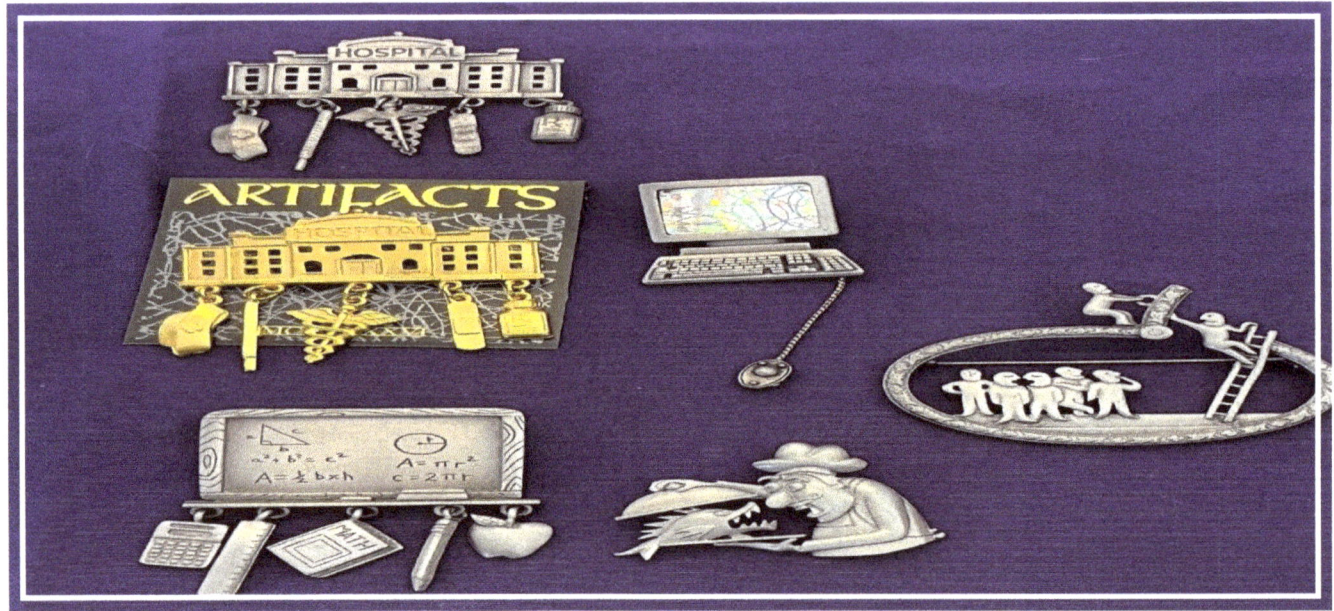

Chef's Surprise pin, designer, Janet Parker Prata

Bugs, butterflies and flowers-ant farm, computer bug, butterfly, beetle and neon pink flower

Bug eating computer, designer, Janet Parker Prata

Celestial, flying, clouds and aliens! The aliens are particularly collectible and bringing high prices on Ebay, Etsy and other websites. Co-author Roesch Rokow loves the cloud and moon pieces, and of course, the aliens!

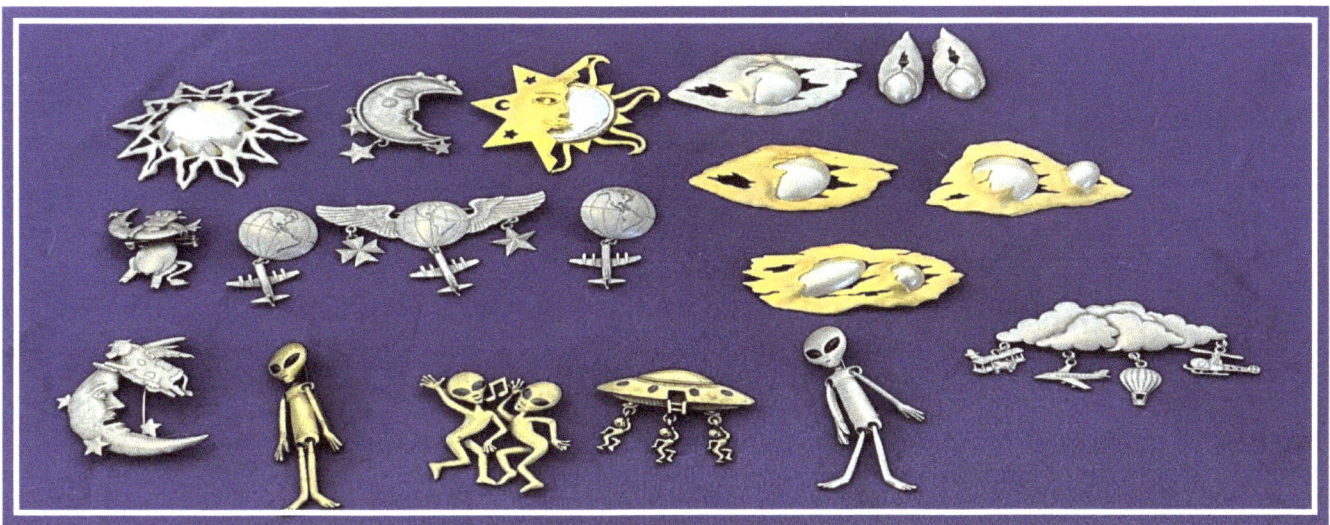

Flights of fancy-birds. The green eyed fellow in the bottom row is a pendant and one of the earliest pieces Roesch Rokow purchased. The burning question is whether the cat in the pin at the top of the picture catches the bird…

Wild animals – cougars, wolves, tigers, cheetahs, lions, porcupines, giraffes, Noah's Ark, gorillas, deer, alligators, elephants, gazelles, zebras, camels, moose, bunnies. The leopard on a log is from 1989 and was designed by Alan Weimer. The giraffe with swirls was designed by Janet Parker Prata
Domestic animals(sort of) cats, pigs, dogs, mice, geese, donkeys, horses, herons, cows

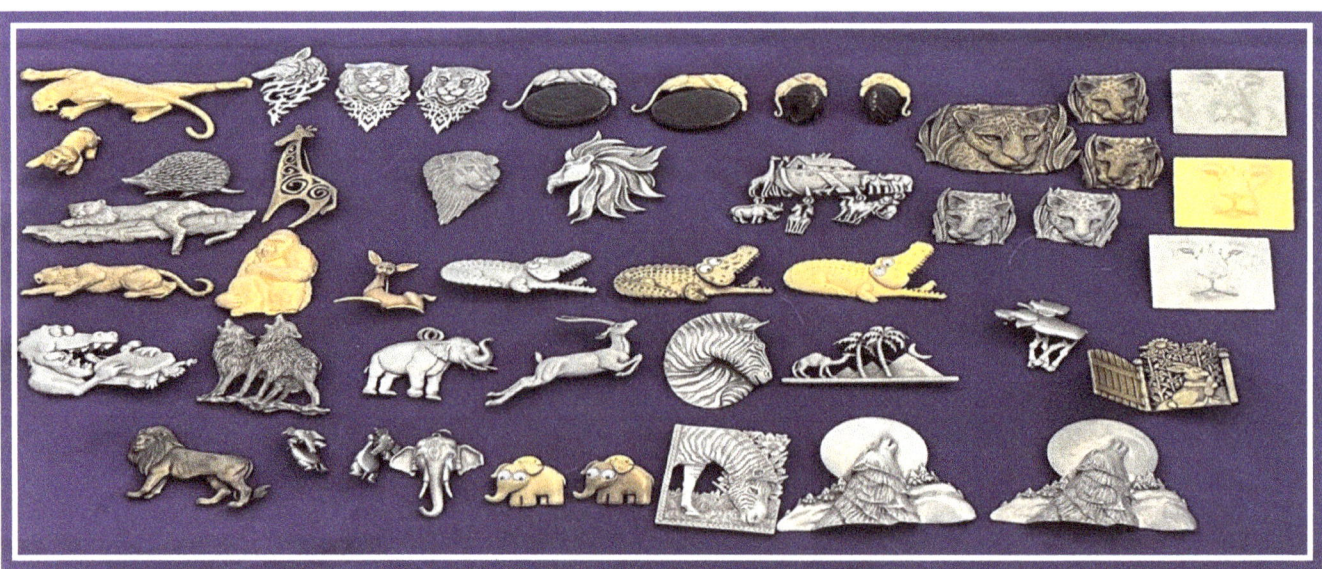

The cat peering in the fishbowl, the cat looking in the mirror and the large cat with the swinging tail are all from 1991, Alan Weimer, designer. The pig with the moveable legs is from 1992. The designer is Alan Weimer. He also created similar pins depicting cows and sheep. The dog slamming the cat into the refrigerator was designed by Ginny Stevens, 1992. Alan Weimer also designed the cat and kitten, goose with the golden egg, the horse in his stall, the two herons and the cow looking up at the moon.

Amphibians and fish. The toad necklace originally came with a simple black cord.

PAGE 173

Dinosaurs and prehistoric times. Isn't the detail amazing? Alan Weimer, designer.

Santa Fe collection-cactus, salamanders, car driving bull, flirting coyotes, adobe houses.
Primitive bar pin top, Janet Parker Prata, designer-dangling charms below, Alan Weimer, designer

The bull standing by the car is from 1990 and the designer, Alan Weimer;

Halloween, Columbus(Indigenous People's) Day, Valentine's Day.
Clock tower with bats, "Boo" ghost and purple rhinestone pin, designer, Janet Parker Prata.

Elegant and Abstract Designs

Janet Parker Prata, designer of the tiger.

Golf bag, Virginia Stevens, designer, 1994 She also designed a golf tee and golf cleat at the same time.

Alan Weimer designs

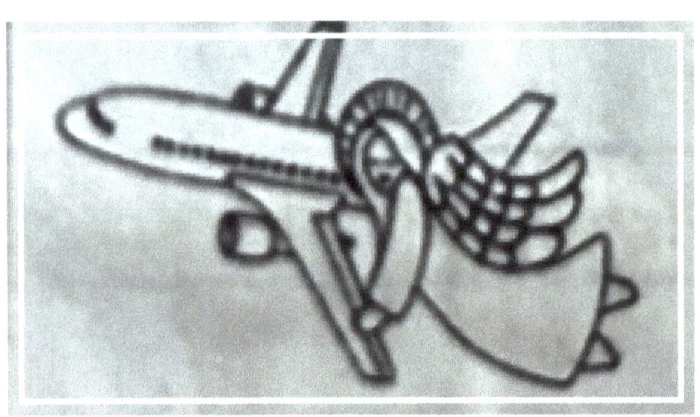

Alan Weimer designs

Alan Weimer designs

Alan Weimer designs

Just like the mighty dinosaurs, JJ's creations will go down in history.

MISCELLANEOUS

PAGE 184

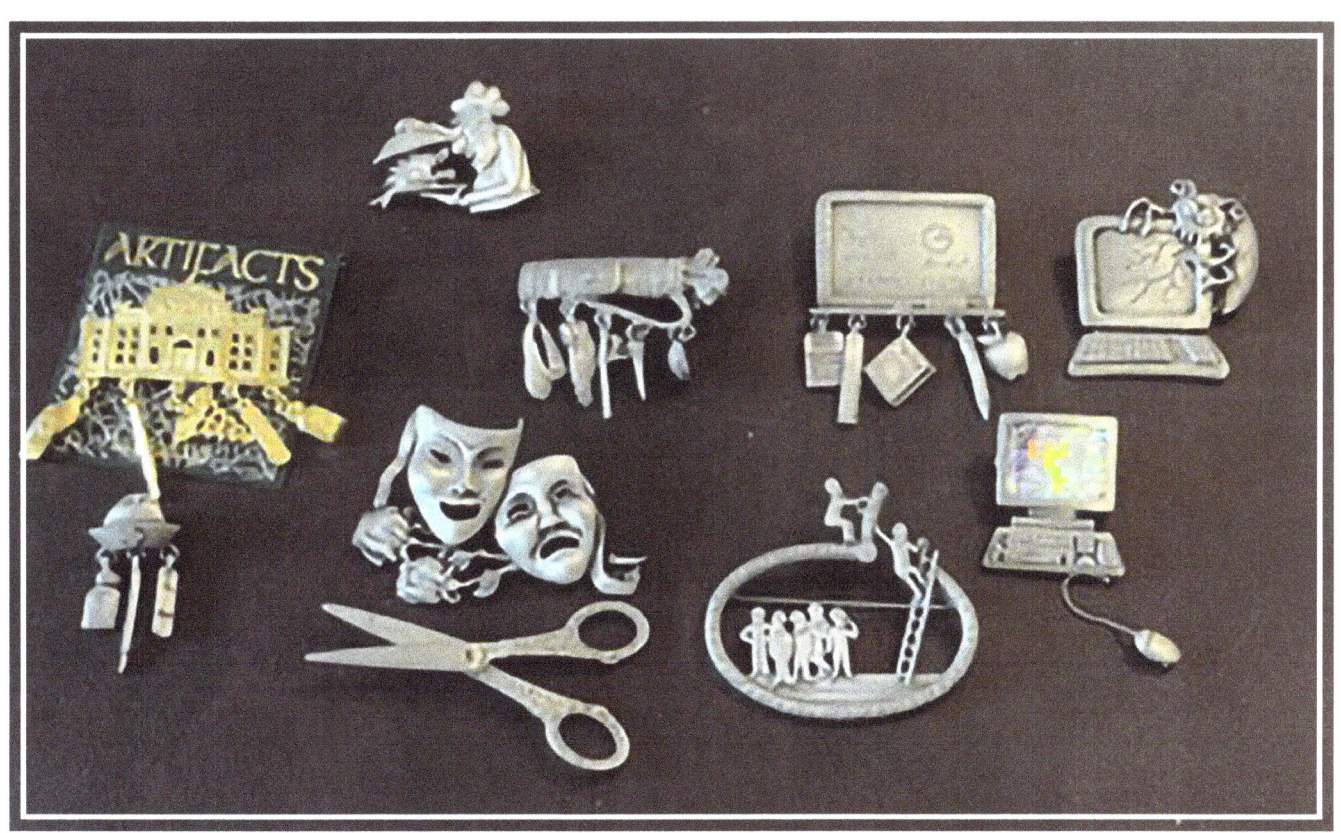

PAGE 186

PAGE 187

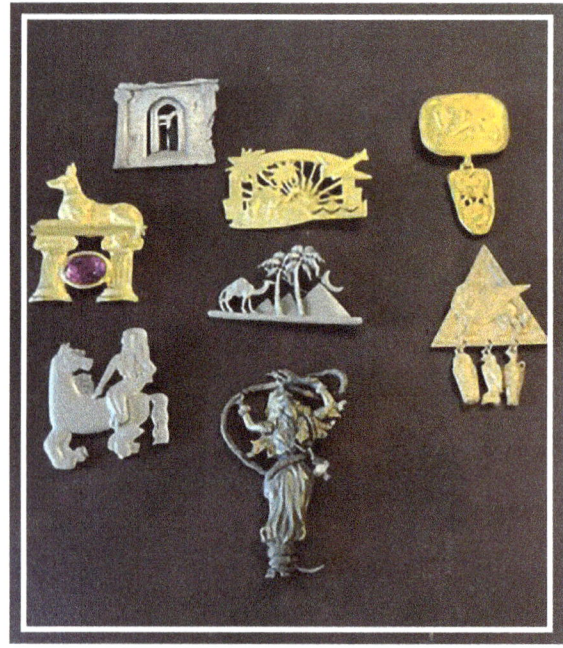

PAGE 188

PAGE 189

PAGE 190

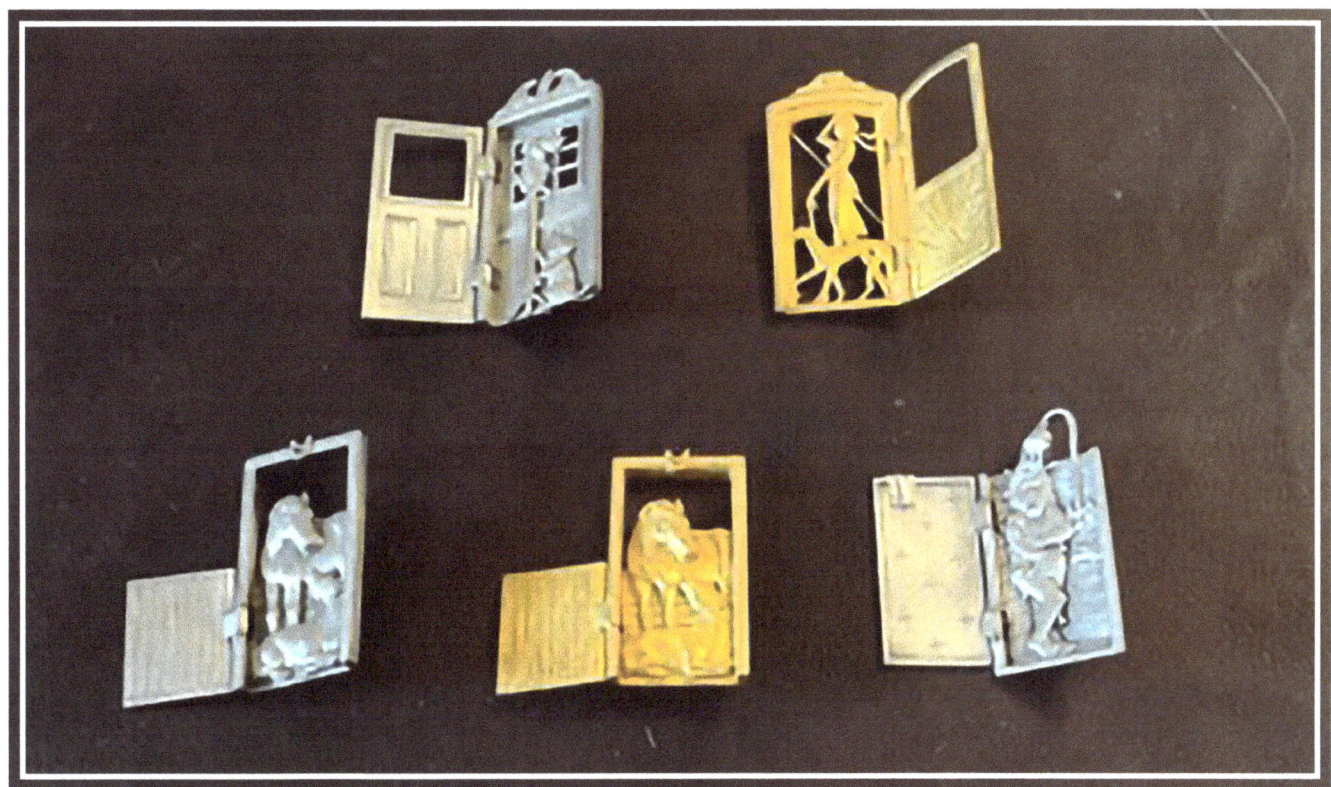

PAGE 191

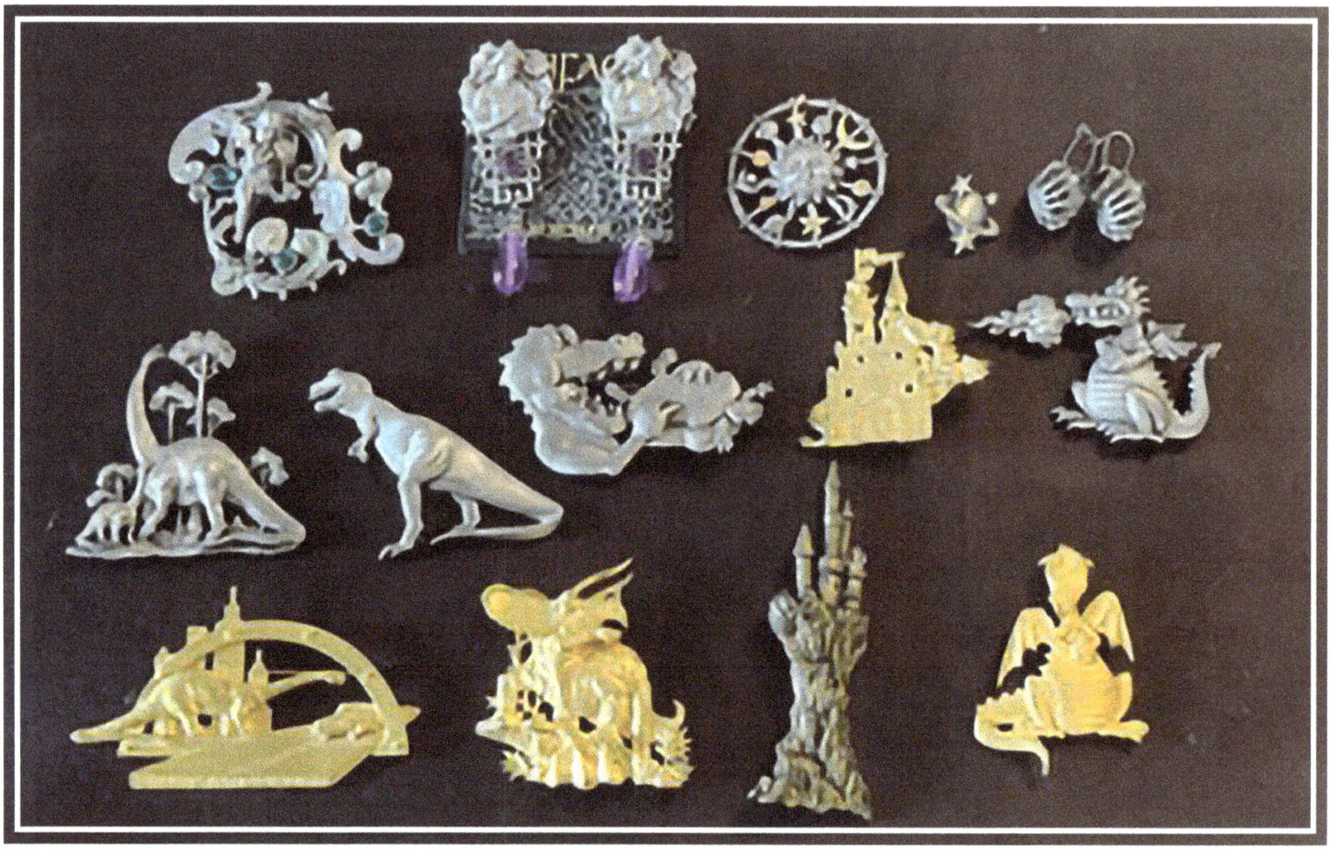

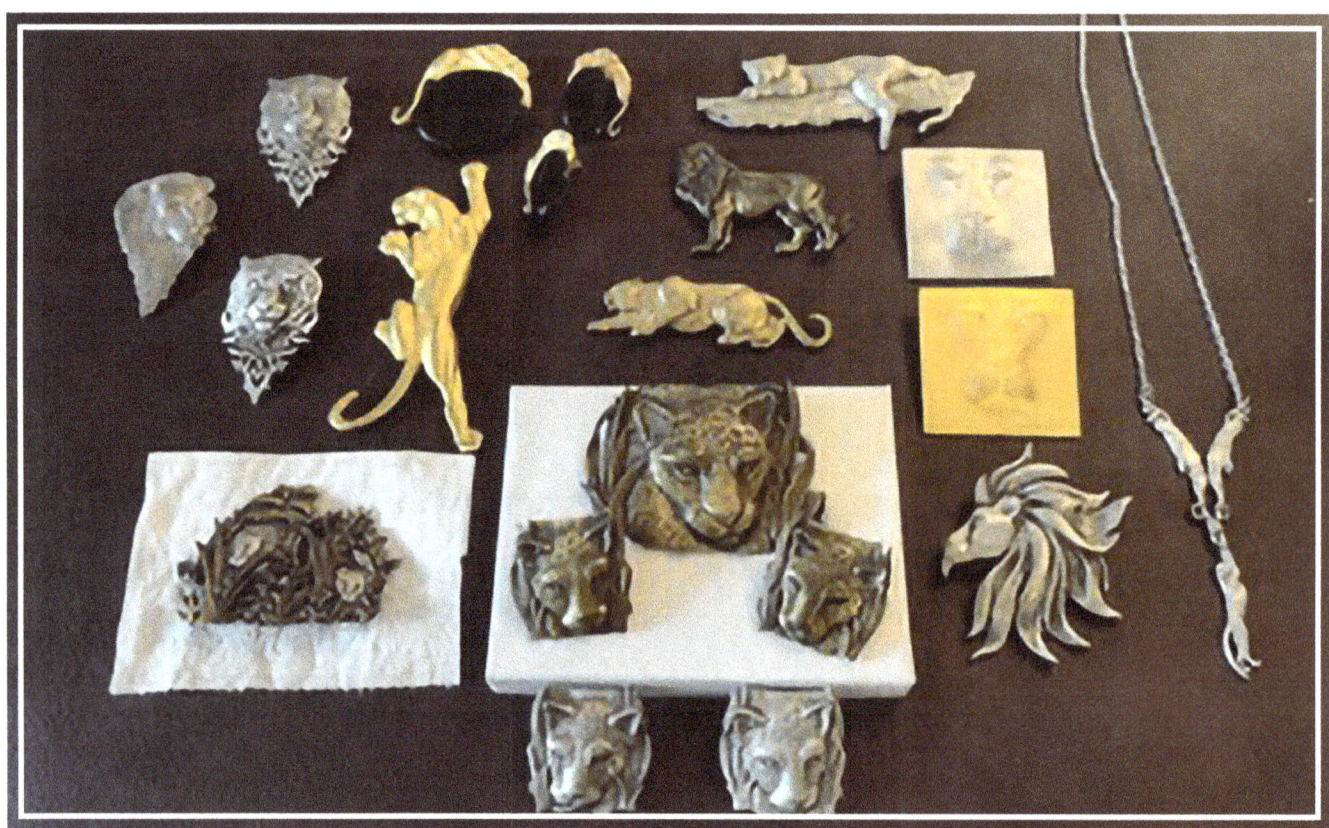

Monkeys in tree and giraffe, designer, Janet Parker Prata

PAGE 193

Ms. Dee designs, necklace came inside the pewter box.

Lovely detail

It says Wooo on the inside

Crystal sculptures Another example of JJ's non-jewelry creations

Picture frames – Although JJ is best known for its wonderful pin designs, the Company made a variety of items, including picture frames like these. These two frames were designed by Janet Parker Prata

Front and Back pictures of the cherry pin

PAGE 197

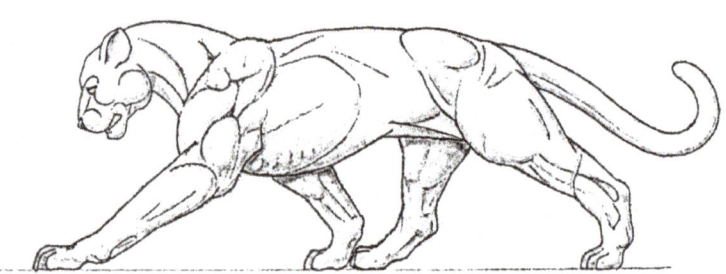

PAGE 200

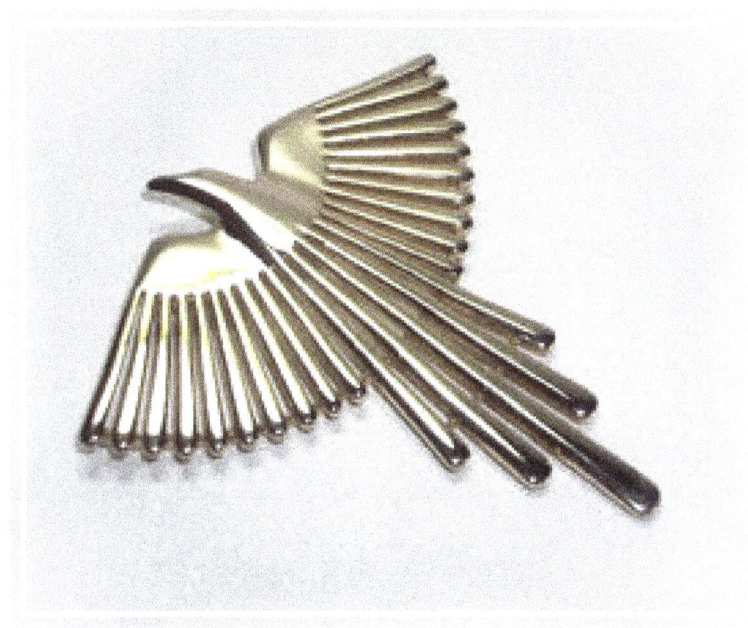

PAGE 203

PAGE 204

PAGE 205

XVI. CONCLUSION

We hope you have enjoyed this journey through the wonderful imagination, creativity and design of the Lisker Family and all the employees of the Jonette Jewelry Company.

INDEX OF SKETCHES

ADVERTISING
A. Poster of different items 154
B. Fruit pin poster 155

AMERICA, AMERICANA – SEE PATRIOTISM

AMPHIBIANS
-frog 40
-frog 41
-frog in circle 41
-frog drinking martini 120
-frog in Santa hat dragging Christmas tree 119
-long legged frog 122
-frog playing flute 120
-frog with umbrella 122
-frog in tub. 123
-frog on lily pad 123
-frog in cattails 123
-toad with flowers 123
-frog in chair 126

ANGELS – SEE RELIGIOUS AND/OR CHRISTMAS

ARKS – SEE RELIGIOUS AND/OR CHRISTMAS

ANIMALS – SEE DOMESTIC ANIMALS, WOODLAND ANIMALS, JUNGLE

AUTUMN/FALL/THANKSGIVING
-acorns 35
-Fall leaves bucket with pumpkins, bird 41
-pumpkin with ornate background 37
-leaf bracelet 128

BIRDS
-penguins 35
-2 birds against cloud 36
-doves against a heart 36
-American eagle 36
-doves and holly wreath 37
-bird with flower 38
-Fall leaves bucket with pumpkins/bird. . . . 41
-flying geese 41
-2 doves with heart between them 38
-cardinal on birdhouse with wreath 125
-Art Nouveau herons quartz clock. 132
-owl quartz clock. 133
-bird perfume bottles 137
-parrot and palm tree 150
-hummingbird (poster) 154
-bird with bird house. 179

BUGS AND BUTTERFLIES
-butterfly 35
-butterfly 35
-butterfly 36
-bumblebee on flower 38
-butterfly 38
-flowers with butterfly 39
-simple butterfly "pretzel" 40
-butterfly in frame 41
-butterfly blue enamel 109
-dragonfly perfume bottle. 155

PAGE 209

CHRISTMAS (ALSO SEE RELIGIOUS)

-tree 35
-doves with holly wreath. 37
-ornament swag. 37
-stockings on mantel. 37,177
-mittens 37
-tree with presents. 38
-"Noel" sign. 39
-bell hanging from bow. 39
-2 skating Santas with string of Christmas
   lights between them. 40
-snowman with shovel 39
-dog with Christmas items in mouths 40
-"graduated steps" tree 41
-geometric Christmas shapes 41
-frog in Santa suit, dragging tree. 119
-round Angel pin. 41
-Merry X-moose 123,160
-Santa face 127
-3 wise men on camels 127
-modern Nativity scene. 127
-cardinal on birdhouse with wreath 125
-snowman against snowflake 125
-Santa. 125,127
-pine trees in snow 125
-Christmas tree box with necklace 130
-teddy bear in Santa hat. 130
-Angel ornament. 142
-Santa in chimney perfume bottle. 137
-Santas 127
-Santa petting dog 153,154
-woman by house with dog. 154
-dog at fireplace with stockings 152
-Christmas cat with mouse 142
-Snowman with star. 143
-Santa boots in chimney 178
-Snowman peering through window 205
-cat in gift box with jingle bell 205
-Santa in chair 202
-Santa holding picture frame. 202

DOMESTIC ANIMALS, FARM

-cat with mouse. 36
-dog running 36
-cat in frame. 38
-bunny in egg. 38
-fancy horse profile 39
-"Eat Veggies" pig, cow, chicken 39
-horse with flowers 39
-dog house "#1 Friend" 38
-dog with bone 38
-cow "I love vegetarians" 40
-dogs carrying Christmas items 40
-side view bunny on leaves 41
-Egyptian cat 41
-cow "kick meat". 41
-3 running horses 39
-Happily Ever After 2 dogs. 39
-cat with flowers on body 38
-dog front and back through doghouse 41
-cat in circle 41
-various cats. 82
-bunny face 107
-various ducks 37,109,117
-duck with surf board. 112
-assorted dogs 114,152-153
-3 dancing mice 114
-3 pigs at trough 110
-tractor. 113

-pigs "making bacon" 116
-pigs with flowers 112,117
-pig with coin (piggy bank) 116
-rooster 113,117
-rocking horse 110
-rooster against sunrise 113
-mouse at hole in wall 118
-galloping horse 111
-dancing pigs 117
-horse with foal (opening door) 117
-woman walking dog (opening door) 117
-hen on Easter eggs 126
-pig napkin ring 128
-animal napkin rings 126,129
-Art Deco cats quartz clock 132
-Scottie dog napkin ring 129
-sleeping cat bookmark 134
-bunny with gate (opening door) 141
-mouse in cabinet (opening door) 139
-Santa petting dog 153-154
-woman with house and dog 154
-cat in window (poster) 154
-Christmas cat with mouse 142
-bunnies on bench 180
-elegant bunny in frame 180
-add to existing "rooster" line 201
-cat in gift box with jingle bell 205
-bunny among flowers 204
-horse with rippling mane 200

EASTER

-bunny in egg 38
-hen on Easter eggs 126

EXPRESSIONS

-"#1 Friend" dog house 38
-"Follow Your Dreams" heart 38
-"Who's Your Daddy!" 38
-nursing expressions 37,38
-"Eat Veggies" with farm animals 39
-"Nurses always care" 38
-cow with "I love vegetarians" 40
-"Nurses are very special people" 40
-love 40
-"I love mom", "I love Grandma" 40
-"Kick meat" cow 41
-This way to my heart, with a $ sign 41
-"Bless All Who Enter This Home" angel
   ornament 142
-born to shop 150
-"dog lover" 152
-bunny with basket 201

FLOWERS/FLORAL – SEE ORNATE DESIGNS

FRUIT/VEGETABLES/LEAVES/TREES/PLANTS

-Apple 40
-Eat Veggies! With picture of farm animals 39
-Cow, with "Kick Meat" 41
-two tone tree 126
-leaf bracelet 128
-grape design spoon or scoop 142
-city skyline with trees 148
-fruit pin poster 155

HALLOWEEN

-bat 35
-witch hat 36
-swirling ghosts 40
-Happy Halloween with bat 41
-pumpkin with mouse in witch hat 41
-ghost with "Boo" 129
-flying witch 127
-creepy witch 150
-jack o lantern 180
-jack o lantern in scarecrow hat 202

HUMOROUS

-chef lifting lid to show fish with teeth ... 117
-3 dancing mice 114
-frog drinking from martini glass 120
-frog in Santa hat, dragging tree 120
-opening door outhouse to reveal man inside 141
-opening door to cabinet to reveal mouse inside 139

JUNGLE/DESERT/SAFARI/OUTBACK/SANTA FE

-Noah's Ark 40,117
-lion profile 40
-koala 40
-tree kangaroo 74
-zebra 106
-monkey 109
-elephant 118
-hippo 107
-hanging ape 111
-alligator 108
-elephant perfume bottles 136
-Noah's Ark perfume bottle 136
-mountain lion or panther (poster) 154
-elephant perfume bottle (poster) 154
-2 lions in underbrush (poster) 154
-various big cats 182
-zebra 203
-giraffe eating vegetation 203
-walking panther 200

LOVE/ROMANCE/VALENTINE'S DAY

-2 doves against a heart 36
-heart 37,41
-"Follow Your Dreams" heart 41
-"The Way to my Heart" with $ sign 41
-floral spray with dangling heart 39
-"I love mom"; "I love Grandma" 40
-Happily Ever After (2 dogs) 39
-ornate rectangle with dangling heart . 41
-2 doves with heart between them 38
-hand palm with heart 38
-2 kids on swing that says "love" . 123,126
-cherub in ornate heart 117

MISCELLANEOUS

-miscellaneous dangles 41
-tractor 113
-Art Deco automobile business card holder 120
-woody car with camper 124
-woody car with canoe 127
-beaded stick pins 130,131
-city skyline perfume bottle 137

- perfume bottle cap designs 138,140
- money in a safe (opening door). 140
- spoon or scoop creation 142
- Red Hat Society dangle pin 143
- woman's hat 146
- Dutch windmill scene 41,147
- city skyline with trees. 148
- antique car 148
- masquerade. 148
- house or church with numbers 150
- beach scenes. 150
- floral chair. 180
- Palm tree scene. 203

MYSTICAL (EGYPTIAN/FANTASY/CELESTIAL/MYTHOLOGY/ALIENS)

- ornate fairy necklace 38
- Egyptian cat 41
- sun and stars. 41
- some mystical pins 98
- Greek key pins 115
- Art Deco Egyptian cats quartz clock 132
- fancy sun. 139
- dragon in oval. 133
- ornate sun quartz clock 133
- sun bookmark 135
- unicorn perfume bottle 136
- sunray perfume bottle 136,137
- sun 137
- woman with stars perfume bottle 138
- castle perfume bottle 138
- dragon magnifying glass pendant 142
- fairies 139,149
- wizards 149
- unicorns 149
- Pegasus 149
- castle. 149
- dragons with castles. 149
- woman with stars in her hair 149
- Art Nouveau woman (poster) 154
- sun (poster). 154
- moon and stars perfume bottle. 155
- add to existing "unicorns" line 200
- sun face. 202

NAUTICAL (LAKE/WATER/OCEAN/ARTIC/BEACH)

- octopus. 35
- penguins 35
- modern dolphin or fish 38
- big mouth fish with teeth 39
- chef lifting lid on fish with teeth. 117
- 3 different lighthouses 121
- seahorse 121
- seashell with wave 39,121-122
- young sailor on boat 123
- lighthouse. 123,126
- dolphins 123
- fish (articulated) 124
- fish 126
- fish napkin ring 128
- lighthouse perfume bottle 137
- fish magnifying glass 142
- sandal bracelet 143
- hat with sunglasses, sandal, swimsuit dangles 143
- women's accessories summer dangle bracelet 143

- beach scene 146,150
- cruise ship with dangles 151
- palm tree scenes 150
- seahorse candle holder 154

OCCUPATIONS – SEE PROFESSIONS

ORNATE DESIGNS, FLORAL, FLOWERS, GENERAL

- flower 35
- flowers 36,38
- flower trio and sunflowers 36
- ornate frame 38
- Celtic design 36
- Celtic cross 38
- big flower pendant 40
- ornate cross pendant 39-40
- flowers 40
- ornate round Celtic design 37
- ornate heart 37,41
- ornate designs 37,38
- bumblebee on flower 38
- flowers with butterfly 39
- Medieval cross 38
- flowers-various 38
- ornate snowflake 39
- flowers in vase 38
- Greek key design 41
- Ornate leaf 41
- sunflowers with leaves 41
- variety of ornate designs 119
- maze pin 115
- spiral "tornado" pin 119
- ornate floral perfume bottles 137

- cherub in ornate heart 117
- ornate Medieval lions with crown 205
- Celtic design 205
- floral locket 204

PATRIOTISM/MILITARY

- USA symbols 36
- map of USA with ange 136
- American eagle 36
- "Don't Mess with the USA" dog tag 36

PEOPLE AND ACCESSORIES

- mother, daughter looking at sun 38
- golfer 40
- woman walking dog (door opens) 117
- 2 kids on swing under "love" 123,126
- Art Nouveau woman quartz clock . . . . .
 . . . . 133, 136, 138, 146
- man in outhouse (opening door) 141
- Art Nouveau woman perfume bottles . .
 136,143,155
- female summer accessories bracelet, pin . 143
- dancing/acrobatic figurines 144-145
- woman's hat 146
- winter accessories 146
- woman with stars in her hair 149
- woman shopping 152-153
- "born to shop" with dangles 146,154
- Art Nouveau woman (poster) 154
- woman walking dog (door opens) 117
- woman with dog 152
- woman perfume bottle 155
- woman with house and dog 154

-young girl with flowers 179
-Art Nouveau women & flapper woman . . 204

PROFESSIONS/OCCUPATIONS/CAREERS

-nursing expressions 37,98
-nursing expressions, medical symbol, cute nurse 38
-nurse expression dog tag 40
-chef with snapping fish 117
-dancing/acrobatic figurines 144-145
-paint palette with painting tool dangles . . 147
-measuring tape with sewing dangles 146
-thimble with needle 151

RELIGIOUS, ANGELS, ARKS

-Celtic cross pendant 38
-"Noel" 39
-ornate cross 40
-angel holding star 149,179
-guardian angel with plane 178
-angel with heart 39,180
-angel carrying flag, blowing trumpet 40
-Noah's ark 40, 117, 180
-3 wise men on camels 127
-modern nativity scene 39,127
-round angel pin 41
-Noah's Ark perfume bottle 136
-angel ornament 142
-church with numbers 150
-St. Francis with animals 152
-add to existing "3 wise men on camels" . . 203
-cross pendant 202
-angel with bird in her hand 200

REPTILES

-alligator 108
-turtle 123
-lizard perfume bottle 155

SAINT PATRICK'S DAY

-3 leaf clover 36
-see also, Celtic designs, under "ORNATE DESIGNS"

SPORTS/GAMING/HOBBIES/ARTS/MUSIC

-golfer 40
-woody car with camper 124
-woody car with canoe 127
-dancers/acrobats 144-145
-skis with dangles 146
-sewing with dangles 146
-"Born to Shop" with dangles 146,150
-paint pallet with dangles 147
-"strike" with bowling pin dangles 147
-two dice keychain 147
-"lucky lady" with gambling dangles 147
-surfboarder under "internet" (surfing the web) 147
-golfbag with golf related dangles 146
-"dance" with dangling ballet slippers 148
-"swing" dancers 148
-thimble, needle 151
-cruise ship with dangles 151
-computer with dangling mouse 151
-gardening dangles, floral top 151

VALENTINE'S DAY – SEE LOVE

WINTER

-ornate snowflake design. 39
-snowman with shove 139
-snowflake 41
-snowman against snowflake 125
-cardinal on birdhouse with wreath 125
-snow pine trees. 125
-snowman with star. 143
-snowman peering through window. 205

WOODLAND ANIMALS/SCENES

-bunny in floral oval frame (egg) 38
-ducks. 37
-flying geese 41
-bunny on leaves 41
-beaver 73
-bunny face 107
-beaver 108
-wolf howling at the moon. 112
-3 bears. 123
-Merry Christ-moose. 123,160
-animal napkin rings 126,129
-bear napkin ring. 129
-howling wolf perfume bottle. 136

INDEX OF JJ PHOTOS

AMERICA, AMERICANA – SEE PATRIOTISM

AMPHIBIANS

- frog book mark 55
- salamander perfume bottle 57
- various frogs 63
- frog earrings 69
- various frogs 95,103
- lizard 103
- frog drinking martini 120
- 2 long-legged frogs 122
- frogs on teeter totter 122
- frog playing flute 120
- frog with umbrella 122
- various amphibians 173,190
- frog in reeds 199

ANGELS – SEE RELIGIOUS AND CHRISTMAS

ARKS – SEE RELIGIOUS AND CHRISTMAS

ANIMALS – SEE DOMESTIC ANIMALS, WOODLAND ANIMALS, JUNGLE

AUTUMN/FALL/THANKSGIVING

- turkey 101,128
- leaves 101,128
- tree 101,128
- scarecrow 101,128
- basket of apples with pumpkins 101,128
- pumpkin 101,128
- haystack 101
- leaf bracelet 101,128
- scarecrow, pumpkin tack pins 101,128
- apple wreath 165,189
- acorns 109

BIRDS

- 2 doves with "Peace", world globe . . 7,98,102
- 2 doves behind Church window (pin opens) 51
- hummingbird perfume bottle 55
- parrot letter opener 66
- stork picture frame 97
- swan on ornate base 95
- eagle in oval frame 102
- 3 other eagles 102
- owls 102
- cardinals 102
- various birds 98,102,172,195
- hummingbird 102
- bird house with Christmas wreath . . 101,128
- loon 112
- doves with heart between them 160
- dove with olive branch 161
- bird watching dangle pin 172
- kiwi bird 172,195
- herons in reeds 173
- peacock on black oval 195
- penguins 195
- bird in birdhouse 199
- feathered bird 199
- owl & pussycat in boat 198
- artistic bird 201

BUGS AND BUTTERFLIES

-dragonfly perfume bottle 57
-bright pink flying bug 86
-bright orange flower with bug 86
-big bug biting computer (computer bug)
    . . . . 171, 185
- lot of various dragonfly, bee and butterfly
    pins 96
-bumblebees 96
-spider with web 96
-hive with bees 96
-ant farm 171,190
-white filigree butterfly 171,190
-pewter beetle 171,190
-green winged bug 190
-butterfly with blue enamel 109

CHRISTMAS (ALSO SEE RELIGIOUS)

-three candles 29
-single candle 29
-wreath with rhinestones 29
-Santa going down chimney perfume bottle 56
-deer, pines, under moon 61,99
-angel holding star 62,162
-angel tack pins 62
-angel earrings 69
-angel letter opener 66
-Christmas bears 97
-Nativity scenes 158
-"NOEL" pin 87,102
-moose,dangling legs 172
-frog dragging Christmas tree 119
-Merry Christmoose with moose 123,160
-Santa face 101,127
-various Christmas pins 158
-Snowman 123,128
-Christmas trees 123,128
-Birdhouse with wreath 101,128
-Snowy pine tree on oval 101,123,128,160
-reindeer profile with holly 101,159
-Woody wagon with Christmas tree on
    top 101,127
-partridge in a pear tree 128
-rhinestone tree 128
-Modern nativity scene 101,127
-3 wise men 101,127,178
-fireplace with stockings 101,178
-full figure Santa with tree 101,127,157
-reindeer helping push Santa up the
    chimney 114,152
-lots of Christmas and religious items 158,189
-doves with heart 160
-dove with olive branch 161
-Christmas bells 161
-Santa boots in chimney 178
-Snowman waving 143

DOMESTIC ANIMALS, FARM

-cat perfume bottle 55
-cat looking out window perfume bottle . . . 57
-circus horse perfume bottle 57
-cat with mouse at his tail 59
-cat carrying kitten 59
-cat going after fish in fishbowl 59
-climbing cat 59
-googly eye cat 59
-cat eyeing birdbath 59
-cat jumping in fishbowl 59

-cat chasing butterfly 59
-cat face with dangling mouse 59
-cat on a swing 59
-tiger cat 59
-cat with ball of yarn 59
-floppy eared dog 60
-backward facing dog with articulating tail . . 60
-Sharpei 60,114
-dog with dish 60
-dog with kitten in basket 60
-googly eyed bulldog 60
-dog with bone 60
-dog with ball 60
-Dalmatian 60
-dog with ball in mouth 60
-crouching Dalmatian 60
-dog with dog related dangles 60
-cat and dog leaning against each other 60
-bone with dog related dangles 60
-initial pins with cats and rhinestones 63
-dog and cat picture frame pins 67
-little girl holding cat 70
-piggy bank pig 70,116
-cat dangling from "mouse error" computer 70
-various domestic animal earrings-cats,
 bunnies, pigs, mice, dogs, cows 69
-Art Deco cat letter opener 66
-cat facing mirror 71,173
-ribbon horse 73
-partial cats (domestic and wild) display 82
-horse with flower in his mouth 87
-cat "bookends" 88
-cow jumping over the moon 90
-cow stuck on the moon 90,171
-dog slamming refrigerator door on cat 90,186

-various farm animals 101
-duck with surf board and other ducks . .
 101,109,112
-horse with flag 109
-roosters 113
-rocking horse 110
-mouse at mouse hole 101,118
-horse 101
-pigs 101
-various domestic and farm animals . . . . .
 101,173,186
-hen with dangling egg 101
-snuggling bunnies 106
-bunny face 107
-pigs at trough 110
-"makin bacon" pigs 110
-galloping horse 111
-angel pig 112
-flowered pig 112
-"dog lover" 114
-3 dancing mice 114
-mice tack pins 114
-pigs 116
-cow "kick meat" 116
-cat, dog, bunny napkin rings 126,129
-mouse in cabinet 139
-various dog pins 114,152-153
-cats with Christmas presents 158
-group of cows 160
-goose laying golden egg 173
-cat on window sill 176
-horse, door opens 173,191
-flying pig over City skyline 166,188
-cow jumping over moon 186

-cat trying to get caged bird (door opens) 172,191
-bunny behind hinged gate (opens) 172
-screeching cat1 77,194
-cat under moon and star 178
-various cat pins. 188,190,194
-3 blind mice 198
-cat playing clarinet 198
-owl & pussycat in boat. 198
-hen with dangling pearl 199
-cat in greenhouse 199
-cat in witch's hat. 203
-rooster 201

EASTER
-hen with Easter eggs 101,123,126
-2 bunnies with Easter basket. . . . 101,123,126
-1 bunny with Easter basket 201

EXPRESSIONS
-"Born to Shop" 64,100
-"nurses make it all better" 65
-"I love nursing" 65
-"Reading" with dangles 68
-"I love teaching" with dangles. 68
-"Teachers Rule" with ruler 68,97-98
-"Favorite Teacher". 68
- "Mom" and "Grandma" picture frame pins, heart lockets. 67
-"I love Grandma" with heart dangle. 70
-"Mouse Error" computer 70,186
-"I love Bingo" 98
-"Very Special Friend" 98

-nursing expressions 96-98
-"Sweet 16", "Happy Sweet 16" w/ car keys 97
-"#1 Mom and #1 Grandma 97
-realtor expressions 97
-"Girl", baby buggy. 97

"ALL YOU NEED IS LOVE"101
-"Love" and "Heart". 101,128
-"Good Day/Bad Day" reversible pin 100
-"I love antiques" 100
-"Bless All Who Enter This Home" ornament 142
-"What's Up" earrings. 184

FLOWERS/FLORAL – SEE ORNATE DESIGNS

FOOD/DINING
-Diner. 34
-coffee lover with dangles 70
-coffee 100
-tea 100
-serving pieces 100
-ice cream. 100
-King of BBQ 100

FRUIT/VEGETABLES/LEAVES/TREES/PLANTS
-leaves. 101
-tree 101,126
-trees against City Skyline 100,148
-cherry pin 184,197

-apple wreath 165
-leaf pins 175
-various flower and leaf pins 184

HALLOWEEN

-skeleton (door opens) 51,175
-creepy hand coming out of jack o' lantern
    mouth 87
-ghosts peering out of dilapidated house. . . 87
-assorted Halloween pins 101,175,194
-ghost pins 187,128
-flying witch 127-128
-ghosts in a graveyard 128
-group of ghosts 165,194
-pumpkin with dangles 175
-bats 175
-skull earrings. 175
-"BOO!" 128
-screeching cat 177,194
-cat under moon and star 178
-skeleton and ghost earrings 184
-spider on web 194
-cat in witch's hat 203

HUMOROUS

-aliens 70,78
-frog sipping from a martini glass . . . 103,120
-cow jumping over moon 90
-gator eating human sandwich 90
-moose with dangling legs 106,193
-dragon flying over City skyline 166,188
-cow stuck on crescent moon 90,186
-dog closing refrigerator door on cat . . 90,186
-big bug eating computer (computer bug) 171
-flirting coyotes 90
-alligator with bird in his mouth (mouth
    opens) 90,104,108,189
-chef lifting lid to see fish with teeth . 166,170
-duck with surf board 101,109,112
-frog in bathtub 103
-mice by martini glass 173
-cat singing. 173
-mice at a bar 173
-cow in herd of longhorn cattle 186
-fishercat and fish going after his tail . 187,194
-coyote smashing car into cactus 187
-cat waiting to hit mouse. 188,194
-surprised woman taking shower (door
    opens) 191

JUNGLE/DESERT/SAFARI/ OUTBACK/SANTA FE

-walking cougar perfume bottle 55
-walking elephant perfume bottle. 55
-2 elephants perfume bottle 56
-howling wolf perfume bottle. 56
-lions perfume bottle. 56
-tiger profile. 58
-2 elephants 58,118
-2 cheetahs. 58
-tiger face. 58,172
-elephant in rectangular frame 58
-"Little Joe" gorilla 58,74,172,193
-crouching panther 58,192
-stalking panther 58,172
-stalking lion and mate 58
-roaring male lion 58

PAGE 221

-lion face 58,172,192
-rhinoceros. 58
-alligator earrings. 69
-elephant earrings 69,107,193
-roaring lion letter opener. 66
-parrot letter opener 66
-tree kangaroo 74,106
-crouching panther over black oval 78,172,192
-partial cat display (both domestic and wild) 82
-lion in oval 85
-moose with dangling legs. 90,107,118,172
-flirting coyotes 90,186
-elephant heads 106-108
-elephant walk 106,118
-2 elephants, trunks up 107,109
-elephant, googly eyes 99,172
-elephant with flowers. 107
-zebra 106,109,172,193
-double elephant tack pin 108
-hippopotamus 107,109,118
-elephant earrings 69,172,193
-Noah's ark. 64,172,193
-monkey earrings. 106-107,109
-assorted jungle animals 99,118,172,192
-hanging ape 111-112
-assorted Santa Fe items 174,186
-mountain lion in brush with flowers. 176,192
-Santa Fe coyote crashing car into cactus. . 187
-steer wearing cowboy hat standing by car 187
-assorted "big cat" jewelry 192
-panther "y" necklace 192
-antelope 193
-monkeys in palm tree. 193
-black enamel antelope 203
-walking panther 200

-female lion looking over her shoulder . . . 200

LOVE/ROMANCE/VALENTINE'S DAY

Heart family picture frame pins 67
-heart with "Love" 101
-heart with "Heart". 101
-envelope with "x's and o's" spilling out .
. . . . 101,175
-palm with heart 101
-children on swing with "love" overhead
. . . . 101,123,126
-open heart design. 191,196
-"love ewe" sheep 175
-various love pins. 191

MISCELLANEOUS

-Gordon's first design, of a peace symbol
   (never made). 11
-Y2K computer pin. 28
-Art Deco vintage car business card
   holder 54,120
-assorted bookmarks. 55,68
-assorted perfume bottles 55-57
-City skyline perfume bottle 57
-circus horse perfume bottle. 57
-initial pins with cats 63
-letter openers 66
-hand with car keys (Sweet 16) 97
-house scene 97
- stick pin 130
-tractor. 109,113
-cars 61,127,174
-masquerade. 100,148

-drama faces 100,147,185
-Red Hat Society hat, people 100,163
-antique car 100,148
-telephone 100,184
-bed 100
-dresser. 100,147
-horse carousel. 100
-"good day/bad day" reversible pin 100
-horse drawn carriage 201

MISCELLANEOUS

-People in hot air balloon 100
-shopping cart 100
-Palm tree scene. 100
-windmill scene 100,147
-City skyline with trees 100,148
-tack pin backs. 148
-spoon or scoop creation 142
-men on a ladder 166,185
-Columbus (Indigenous People's) Day
    world, dangles. 175,184
-City skylines 166,188
-Artifacts card 171
-Dinosaurs 166,174,181,192
-money tree 184
-couple behind car. 184
-cloud with transportation dangles. 187
-Big Bad Wolf (door opens) 198
-3 Blind Mice 198
-Humpty Dumpty 198
Owl & Pussycat in boat 198

MYSTICAL (EGYPTIAN/FANTASY/ CELESTIAL/MYTHOLOGY)

-Anubis Egyptian pin, purple stone . . . . .
    19,166,188
-sun bookmark 55
-Castle with dragon perfume bottle 56
-Unicorn perfume bottle. 56
-Pegasus perfume bottle 56
-Sunray perfume bottle 55,57
-Crescent moon and stars perfume bottle . . 57
-Fairy perfume bottle 57
-Pegasus with blue sparkles. 62
-Fairy with wand 62
-Sun with stars, moons, planets pin, ear-
    rings 62,86,93
-Cascading stars, pin, earrings. 62
-Fairy child sitting on crescent moon. 62
-kissing sun and crescent moon 62
-star and moon earrings 62
-cow jumping over the moon earrings 69
-long, articulated alien 70,78
-2 aliens, peering through window 70
-3 aliens, dangling from spaceship 70,78
-sun letter opener 66
-Art Deco Egyptian cat letter opener. 66
-sun and stars mirror. 71
-dancing aliens 78
-figures dancing under moon 78
-colored Saturn 78
-profile of a woman against sun and
    moon. 86,169
-Egyptian Art Deco "bookend" cats 88
-dragon with crystal ball, blue glitter 92
-wizard holding scepter. 94
-Pegasus .92,149-150

-dragon in front of castle 92,149,187
-fairy by crescent moon 91
-trio of mystical tack pins 93
-fairy with wand and blue glitter 94
-unicorn with blue glitter 92
-woman against crescent moon pendant . . . 93
-mystical charm bracelet 93
-Medieval lionor Griffin 92
-sun,moon,planets,stars pin 93
-sun 96
-fairy on a cloud 91
-castle 92
-fairy on a pearl oval 94
-Art Deco female face 93
-fairy with flowers 91
-Griffin 99
-dragon in oval 99
-Sphinx 99-100
-early Egyptian figure 99-100
-Dimensional star 99-100
-Cloud with thunderbolts 97
-various ornate and Medieval designs . . 98,115
-various designs 99-100,167
-unicorn pins 99,179
-dragon with blue dangle 104
-winged bull with flower 104
-crescent moon and stars 105
-Greek key design pins (spirals) 115
-wizards 149-150
-unicorns 149-150
-fairies 149-150
-Celestial picture frame 197
-Pegasus crystal figurine 196
-dragon magnifying glass 142

-various mystical pins . . . .
 167-168,185,187-188,192,195
-Art Deco Egyptian prone cat 166
-mysterious figure in ruins 166,188
-flying dragon over City skyline 166,188
-flying saucer over City skyline 90,166,188
-display of assorted cloud, celestial, alien,
 aviation pieces 171
-unicorn with dangle 179
-sun and crescent moon with aurora borealis cabochons 181
-cloud with transportation dangles 187
-aliens 171
-cloud,moon and sun pieces 115,171,185
-Lady Godiva 188
-add to existing "unicorn pins" 200
-sun face 202
-artistic dragon 202
-artistic winged gargoyle 201

NAUTICAL (LAKE/WATER/OCEAN/ARTIC/BEACH)

-2 fish perfume bottles 56,57
-searay 63
-manatee earrings 69
-penguin earrings 69
-lighthouses 95,103,121,122
-manatee with baby 173,189
-shell with surf 103,121-122
-young sailor "seek new horizons" . . . 103,123
-seahorses 95,121
-mermaid 95,177,195
-big fish with teeth and bug-eyes 95
-seashel 195,103

-ship, sailboat 95
-various lighthouses and boats 103,121
- dolphins 95
-fish magnifying glass 142
-beach scene 146
-chef with snapping fish 166,170
-lighthouse tack pins 173
-fish 173
-fishercat with fish going after his tail 187-188
-various fish and lighthouses 189
-primitive fish 205
-shells in sand 204

OCCUPATIONS – SEE PROFESSIONS

ORNATE DESIGNS, FLORAL, FLOWERS, GENERAL

-floral perfume bottle 57
-flower wagon 70
-flowers in vase 70
-crown bar pinwith wing dangle 84
-bright orange flower with bug 86
-fancy antique key with dangles 97
-fanciful dragons 92
-woman's face 93
-Greek key designs 115
-swirl "tornado" pin 119
-stick pin 130
-various flower pins 96
-ornate dangle earrings 98,102
-various ornate and Medieval designs . . . .
. . . . 98-100,102
-various ornate designs and earrings . 102,175
-spiral snake pin 165

-various ornate designs 169
-various ornate designs 175,184-185
-fan design with crystal 169,184
-bright pink flower 171
-ornate mermaid pin 177,195
-bright yellow flower 199
-colorful flowers 199
-change page on existing "bright yellow
    flower" 207
-primitive rectangular design 205
-Celtic design pin 205
-ornate pendant 204

PATRIOTISM/MILITARY

-world globe with plane dangles, angel
    wings 84,171,187
-rhinestone flag pin 97
-eagle in oval frame 102
-2 doves holding world between them, with
    peace banner 98,102
-horse with American flag 109
-eagle pin 176

PEOPLE AND ACCESSORIES

-teacher bookmarks 55
-Art Nouveau woman perfume bottle . . 55,56
-dancing couple perfume bottle 57
-Art Nouveau kneeling woman perfume
    bottle 57
-"Mom" and "Grandma" lockets and pic-
    ture frame pins 67
-Stork holding baby picture frame 67

-child picture frame pin with dangling "Baby" 67
-teacher in front of class 68
-"I love Grandma" with heart 70
-little girl holding a cat 70
-baby earrings 69
-woman letter opener 66
-female picture frame 71
-Art Nouveau female profile 72
-woman against a crescent moon 86,169
-Art Deco female face 93
-2 young profiles facing each other 97
-stork dangling picture frame for baby 97
-various Mom and Grandma pins 97
-Asian woman face 98,168,184
-Picasso style face 98-99
-women flapper tack pins 100
-children on swing, "LOVE" 101,126
-dancing figurines 144-145
-ribboned hat 146
-female forms, including Red Hat Society
  100,163,191,195
-people dancing under a moon 78,169
-woman flowered dress with dog 152-153
-couple running with dog 153
-men on ladder 166
-people by skylines 166,188
-woman in pearl bubble bath 170
-more female forms, including Art Nouveau 170,184
-Lady Godiva 170
-children on playground 170
-woman walking dog (door opens) ... 170,191
-girl on bike 187

-surprised woman taking shower (door opens) 191

PROFESSIONS/OCCUPATIONS/CAREERS

-teacher bookmarks 55
-realtor sign with dangles 65,97,98
-mirror with dangles (hairdresser) 65,97
-hospital with dangles ... 65,76,87,166,170,185
-secretary/administrative assistant at desk .. 65
-"God Bless" secretary or administrative assistant 65
-"Nurses make it better" 65,87
-"For Sale" realtor sign 65,97,98
-Sewing with dangles 65
-toothbrush with dangles (dentist, dental hygienist) 65
-nurse's cap, dangles, earrings and pin ...
  65,88,98,185
-hand with manicurist dangles 65
-"I love nursing" with dangles 65,85
-various teaching items 68
-computer with dangling mouse ....
  70,151,166,170,185
-"mouse error" computer 70
-bank with dangling pennies 70,96
-pig with penny in slot (piggy bank) 70
-swing dancers 84
-sock hop dancers 84
-nurse angel 85,96
-chefs 96,166
-realtors 96-97
-nursing 96-97
-secretary, administrative assistant 96-97
-hairdressers/beauticians 97

-"teachers rule" 97
-chalkboard with dangles 97,166,170,185
-real estate bracelet 96,98
-chef with snapping fish 96,166,170,185
-various professions 104
-bug eating computer 185
-scissors 185
-swing couple. 199

RELIGIOUS, ANGELS, ARKS

-2 doves in Church window (opens). 51
-angel holding star. 62,162,179
-angel tack pins 62
-angel earrings 69
-angel letter opener 66
-nurse angel 85
-nativity scene 88,158
-modern nativity scene 29,88,101,127
-"NOEL" pin 87
-Noah's Ark pin and earrings 64,172,193
-3 wise men on camels 101,127,178
-angel blowing her horn, holly 101
-various crosses 102
-angel ornament 142
-St. Francis with animals 152
-various Christmas and religious items 158,189
-angel trinket box 176
-"3 wise men on camels" 203

REPTILES

-alligator earrings. 69,103,122
-alligator with bird in mouth (opens) . . . .
. 90,99,104,189
-gator eating human sandwich 90
-snakes 99
-swimming turtle. 103
-turtles 103,122,173,189
-walking turtle 103
-spiral snake pin. 165

SPECIALTY

-J. Benton "Duh" face pin 20
-J. Benton "You So Crazy" face pin 20
-Spoontiques mirror with dangles 21
-Spoontiques Angel pin. 21
-Ms. Dee cat trinket box with jewelry. 23
-Ms. Dee sailboat trinket box with jewelry. . 23
-Ms. Dee owl trinket box with jewelry . 22,196
-crystal figurines 196

SPORTS/GAMING/HOBBIES/ARTS/MUSIC

-camping related items 61,100
-musical notes with dangling instruments . . 64
-tennis racquet with dangling related items . 64
-shopping pin with dangles. 64,146
-"DANCE" with ballerina shoe dangles .
. . . . 64,100,148
Thimble with thread 64,147
-ballerina shoe earrings 64
-bowling. 64,100,147
-skis with dangles. 64,100,146,187
-golf bag with dangles. . . . 64,100,146,177,185
-watering can with dangles 64
-retro sled. 64
-sewing with dangles 65,146
-mirror with hairdressing dangles. 65

-hand with manicure dangles 65
-computer with dangling mouse. . . 70,151,185
-"Mouse error" computer. 70,100
-swing dancers. 100,148
-golf picture frame 197
-BBQ 100
-cruise ship with dangles. 100
-masquerade. 100
-skating. 100
-shopping cart 100
-gambling. 100,147
-drama faces. 100,185
-piano. 100
-computers. 70,100,170,185
-I love antiques 100
-people in hot air balloon 100
-dancers, acrobats 100,144-145
-ethnic dancer with scarf 100
-internet surfer. 100,147
-paint pallet 147
-girl on bicycle 187
-saxophone 202

VALENTINE'S DAY – SEE LOVE

WINTER

-deer, pines under moon. 61,99
-moose in oval frame. 61
-moose, dangling legs, earrings. 90,99
-evergreen with snow on oval. 101,128
-snowman 143

WOODLAND ANIMALS/SCENES

-moose against trees 61
-2 howling wolves 61,172,193
-deer, pines, under moon 61
-bears climbing tree. 61
-canoe with camping related dangles 61
-bear. 61
-canoe earrings with compass, oar dangles . 61
-woody car with canoe 61
-vintage station wagon towing camper. 61
-cute bear with pencil 68
-teddy bear earrings (2 kinds) 69
-bunny earrings 69
-racoons picture frame 71
-cute bear on swing. 97
-cute bear frame with mirror 97
-bear on snow sled 97
-bear earrings and other bear items 97
-some woodland animals. 99
-bunny face 107
-howling wolf 108,112,172,193
-wolf profile. 108
-moose. 90,106,172,193
-deer, woodland scene. 61
-2 bunnies 99,106
-beaver 108,112
-Mama bear, baby bear tack pins 106
-bear napkin ring 126,129
-deer. 172,193
-porcupine 193
-beaver with chain saw 193
-sleeping bear. 193

www.ingramcontent.com/pod-product-compliance
Lightning Source LLC
Chambersburg PA
CBHW042351070526
44585CB00028B/2896